THE UNUSABLE PAST

Scholars Press
Studies in the Humanities

THE UNUSABLE PAST
America's Puritan Tradition, 1830 to 1930

Jan C. Dawson

Scholars Press
Chico, California

THE UNUSABLE PAST
America's Puritan Tradition, 1830 to 1930

Jan C. Dawson

© 1984
Scholars Press

Library of Congress Cataloging in Publication Data

Dawson, Jan C.
  The unusable past.

  (Scholars Press studies in the humanities series ; no. 4)
  1. Puritans—United States—History. 2. United States—
Intellectual life. I. Title. II. Series.
BX9354.2.D39   1984   285'.9'0973   83-27091
ISBN 0-89130-721-4
ISBN 0-89130-722-2 (pbk.)

Printed in the United States of America

CONTENTS

To My Family

Acknowledgments

Having begun this study ten years ago as a doctoral dissertation, I have received more assistance than I could ever fully acknowledge. The University of Washington History Department, McNeese State University, and Southwestern University provided financial support at various stages that was indispensable. Because all of the sources for the work are published sources and come from over a hundred-year time span, the interlibrary loan staffs of the University of Washington and Southwestern University performed an especially valuable service. Although it is primarily a teaching institution, Southwestern facilitated the final preparation of the book in many other ways as well, most particularly in the very professional and always good-natured secretarial assistance provided by Kathy Buchhorn and Dottie Secor, both of whom, along with Christy Dawson, also helped with proofreading. At Scholars Press, John Crowell, Mary Bishop and Kim Weir made the publication process seem to me much smoother than it really is.

My intellectual indebtedness begins with early graduate school debates with Michael Doyle, Susan Frey, and Mott Greene, all of whom commented on the earliest conceptualizations of this study, about the nature of intellectual history, and particularly about ideas as elusive as those alleged to be associated with the Puritan tradition. Perhaps more convinced than they that what Americans have meant by the Puritan tradition could be systematically studied were Otis Pease and Thomas Pressly, who gave the work very careful and perceptive readings at the dissertation stage and who have continued to provide encouragement to press on with the book. Similar encouragement after partial readings of the manuscript came from Joe Gray Taylor, and, at an especially crucial stage, Weldon Crowley. Most recently, T. Walter Herbert gave the manuscript a complete and exceptionally thorough reading, the stylistic and conceptual benefits of which will go far beyond this particular work. Although each of these readers would undoubtedly have written a different book than I have, I am indebted to them for much of what I hope is worthwhile in this one.

This is even more true of Lewis O. Saum. He not only entrusted to me a topic in which he had no small measure of interest, but he has also patiently, sensitively, and always good-humoredly helped me to see more clearly what I have discovered about it. He has read and commented on the manuscript at every stage; but most importantly, he has provided a congenial model for doing intellectual history that treats respectfully, though certainly not uncritically, what people who have cared enough to put their ideas down in writing have thought.

Chapter 5 originally appeared as "The Puritan and the Cavalier: The South's Perception of Contrasting Traditions," *Journal of Southern History*, 44 (November 1978), 597–614. Reprinted by permission of the Managing Editor.

Chapter 6 originally appeared as "Puritanism in American Thought and Society: 1865–1910," *New England Quarterly*, 53 (December 1980), 508–26. Reprinted by permission.

Introduction

In *Democracy in America*, first published in 1835, the French author Alexis de Tocqueville wrote:

> The chances of birth favored the Americans; their fathers of old brought to the land in which they live that equality both of conditions and of mental endowments from which, as from its natural source, a democratic republic was one day to rise. But that is not all; with a republican social state they bequeathed to their descendants the habits, ideas and mores best fitted to make a republic flourish. When I consider all that has resulted from this first fact, I think I can see the whole destiny of America contained in the first Puritan who landed on these shores, as that of the whole human race in the first man.[1]

A century later, in 1936, the Spanish-American philosopher George Santayana published *The Last Puritan*, "A Memoir in the Form of a Novel" about Oliver Alden who embodied "Puritanism Self-condemned." When, in the prologue, Santayana defines Puritanism as "a natural reaction against nature," his friend Mario Van de Weyer tries to convince him to write Oliver's history because "in Oliver puritanism worked itself out to its logical end." Oliver insisted that "[w]e have dedicated ourselves to the truth, to living in the presence of the noblest things we can conceive. If we can't live so, we won't live at all." Oliver did die, in a world war in which he did not believe, but not before, according to Mario, "he convinced himself, on puritan grounds, that it was wrong to be a puritan." The last Puritan convinced himself, that is, that being a Puritan was no longer among the noblest things.[2]

The times and places that separate these two familiar but radically different judgments on American Puritanism reveal much about the history of the Puritan tradition. Tocqueville's France had recently experienced one of those revolutions that tried unsuccessfully to install stable self-government resembling what the United States, ostensibly because of the Puritan tradition, seemed to have achieved so effortlessly. The New England to which the Madrid-born Santayana came after the Civil War

---

[1] Alexis de Tocqueville, *Democracy in America*, ed. George Lawrence (Garden City, N.Y.: Doubleday and Company, Inc., Anchor Book, 1966), 279.

[2] George Santayana, *The Last Puritan* (New York: Charles Scribner's Sons, 1935), 6, 582.

to be educated, and later to educate, had seen its moral and intellectual leadership of the United States gradually fade away in the preceding half-century and a modernistic, pluralistic, secular culture begin to take its place. Tocqueville's generation in America believed even more strongly than he that the first Puritans had brought with them the destiny of the United States, although not all of them agreed that that destiny was especially favored. Santayana's American contemporaries agreed with him that it was wrong to be Puritan, although few of them tried to understand why as scrupulously as he did. Throughout the century from the 1830s to the 1930s Americans, no less than non-Americans, wrestled with the meaning of Puritanism for the development of the United States. In contrast to when non-Americans made them, however, such exertions by Americans constituted participation in the very life, and ultimately in the death, of the Puritan tradition.

This book is about the largely self-conscious remaking of America's Puritan tradition, beginning with the romantic revival of interest in Puritanism around 1830, and its equally self-conscious unmaking, ending around 1930. The description and analysis of this process is based on the writings of those articulate Americans who wrestled publicly with the meaning of Puritanism in the elevated journals and other published materials of the period. Their works display not merely rhetorical uses of the designation *Puritan*, such as the early nineteenth-century identification of New England upper-class genealogy with the Puritan legacy; nor preoccupation with behavioral and thematic similarities between the colonial and national periods, such as the Protestant work ethic. What they do show are serious and explicit efforts to understand the Puritan inheritance, to adapt it to current issues, to revise it, to critique it, and finally to make it serve the rapid expansion of American society and culture. The extent and seriousness of these efforts very early convinced me that, Darrett Rutman's contention in the preface to *American Puritanism* notwithstanding, Puritanism is not and never has been primarily a historian's concept.[3] It may have become that to late twentieth-century scholars, and indirectly this study addresses why. But the Puritanism debated by concerned Americans from 1830 to 1930 had been to them a very real part of colonial life and continued to be a very real presence in the life of the young nation, even when it appeared as an ogre or as a ghost.

Acknowledging the considerable methodological difficulties involved, this study nevertheless assumes that both Puritanism and the Puritan tradition were authentic historical phenomena and historical forces. It proceeds on this assumption by finding the Puritan tradition in specific reflections upon it, in what people writing, as far as I could tell, in good

---

[3] Darrett Rutman, *American Puritanism: Faith and Practice* (New York: J. B. Lippincott, Co., 1970), Preface.

faith about Puritanism, said it was. Thus, it resembles analyses of an early component of the Puritan tradition, Calvinist theology, in such diverse works as Joseph Haroutunian's *Piety versus Moralism* (1932) and Ann Douglas's *The Feminization of American Culture* (1977), more than existing studies of the Puritan legacy. Although Puritanism, as distinct from Calvinism, did not consist of five propositions whose transformation can be systematically traced, it did have more a core and more continuity than some students of the Puritan tradition have indicated. Scholars of the 1940s, 1950s, and early 1960s, for example, defined the Puritan tradition so broadly it was difficult to imagine what in American life was not influenced by Puritanism. Although Ralph Barton Perry's *Puritanism and Democracy* (1944) tried to avoid the pitfalls of overgeneralizing the meaning of Puritanism, the work set the tone for viewing Puritanism in abstract rather than concrete terms. *The Puritan Heritage* (1952) by George M. Stephenson, *Yankees and God* (1954) by Chard Powers Smith, and *The Puritan Heritage: America's Roots in the Bible* (1964) by Joseph Gaer and Ben Siegal, were less philosophical and more historical treatments than *Puritanism and Democracy*. But each in its own way considered the Puritan tradition as, in the words of Chard Powers Smith, "a sub-conscious psychological system," which, by some mysterious mechanism, shaped American attitudes and institutions. Sacvan Bercovitch's *The Puritan Origins of the American Self* (1975) and *The American Jeremiad* (1978) remove some of the mystery from this process. But even they do more to construct a Puritan tradition for modern students to contemplate than to reconstruct a legacy believed by past generations sometimes to inspire and other times to obstruct national development.[4]

On the other hand, recent historians of the colonial period have defined Puritanism so narrowly that whatever traces of the Puritan tradition they find after the early eighteenth century appear as isolated instances, unrelated to any general habits of national thought or practice. Francis J. Bremer's *The Puritan Experiment* (1976), James W. Jones's *The Shattered Synthesis: New England Puritanism before the Great Awakening* (1973), Darrett Rutman's *American Puritanism: Faith and Practice* (1970), and Larzer Ziff's *Puritanism in America: New Culture in a New World* (1973) follow the trend of the late 1960s of viewing

---

[4] Joseph Haroutunian, *Piety versus Moralism* (New York: Harper and Row, Publishers, Inc., Harper Torchbook, 1970); Ann Douglas, *The Feminization of American Culture* (New York: Avon Books, 1977), chap. 4; Ralph Barton Perry, *Puritanism and Democracy* (New York: Vanguard Press, 1944); George Stephenson, *The Puritan Heritage* (New York: Macmillan Co., 1952); Chard Powers Smith, *Yankees and God* (New York: Hermitage House, 1954), chap. 7; Joseph Gaer and Ben Siegal, *The Puritan Heritage: America's Roots in the Bible* (New York: New American Library, Mentor Books, 1964); Sacvan Bercovitch, *The Puritan Origins of the American Self* (New Haven: Yale University Press, 1975) and *The American Jeremiad* (Madison: Univ. of Wisconsin Press, 1978).

Puritanism in pluralistic terms, rejecting the notion elaborated by Perry Miller, for example, that Puritanism was the product of a single, unified, monolithic intelligence. Whether the focus be Puritan culture, Puritan ideology, Puritan fellowship, or the Puritan synthesis, however, these works conclude that Puritanism disintegrated at the time of the Great Awakening. Colonial Puritanism may indeed have disintegrated by the mid-eighteenth century, if not earlier, but its original elements did not necessarily lose their ability to guide and mold American civilization; and, according to nineteenth-century commentators, those elements were not quite as fragmented as current historiography contends.[5]

The core and the continuity of the Puritan tradition begin to emerge for the historian to see most clearly when New England Calvinism began to decline and, simultaneously, the differentiation of Calvinism and Puritanism accelerated. The conventional date for the beginning of the end of New England Calvinism's cultural hegemony is the 1805 appointment of Henry Ware, a Unitarian rather than a Calvinist theologian, to the prestigious Hollis Professorship of Divinity at Harvard College. The appointment intensified and further institutionalized a split in New England's religious culture going back at least to Jonathan Edwards's orthodox refutation of Arminianism in the second quarter of the eighteenth century and perpetuated by the diffusion of deistic rationalism after mid-century. Embodied in the controversy between Calvinists and Unitarians after 1805, the split in the religious culture of New England paradoxically fostered on another more secular level a new unity and self-consciousness about the region's civic culture and its place in history. The revival of interest in Puritanism was a primary manifestation of this development. Calvinists claimed the Puritan legacy on doctrinal grounds, symbolized by the Reverend Lyman Beecher naming his Calvinist journal *The Spirit of the Pilgrims* in 1827; and Unitarians insisted that their emerging ecclesiastical, civil, and cultural leadership made them the true heirs of the Puritan theocracy.[6]

[5] Francis J. Bremer, *The Puritan Experiment* (New York: St. Martin's Press, 1976); James W. Jones, *The Shattered Synthesis: New England Puritanism before the Great Awakening* (New Haven: Yale Univ. Press, 1973); Rutman, *American Puritanism*; Larzer Ziff, *Puritanism in America: New Culture in a New World* (New York: Viking Press, 1973). The following essays are especially helpful in presenting the problem of defining Puritanism and the nature of the Puritan legacy: Michael McGiffert, "American Puritan Studies in the 1960's," *William and Mary Quarterly*, 3d series, 27 (January 1970): 36–37, for the monolithic vs. pluralistic approaches; Norman Petit, "The Puritan Legacy," *New England Quarterly* 48 (June 1975): 283–94; Richard Schlatter, "The Puritan Strain," in *The Reconstruction of American History*, ed. John Higham (London: Hutchinson University Library, 1962), 22–45; and George M. Waller's Introduction to *Puritanism in Early America* (Boston: Heath, 1950), v–x.

[6] In addition to Haroutunian, *Piety versus Moralism* and Douglas, *The Feminization of American Culture*, also helpful are Henry May, *The Enlightenment in America* (New

An important feature of this controversy was the republication of seventeenth-century Puritan tracts selected to support the respective claims of the Calvinists and Unitarians, but in the end making an even more important contribution to the generally greater interest in the past associated with the romantic period. Reinforcing this historical interest in the Puritans was the national bicentennial celebration of the landing of the Pilgrims at Plymouth Rock in 1620. In preparation for that celebration residents of New England, and New Englanders who had emigrated to other parts of the United States, organized New England societies, modeled on the Old Colony Club and its successor, the Pilgrim Society, at Plymouth.[7] Daniel Webster's famous Plymouth Oration was only one of many eulogies to the Pilgrims and Puritans delivered that December, 1820. The increasing availability of material about the Puritan past also influenced the literary popularization of Puritanism. A serial on "Salem Witchcraft" in the *New York Literary Journal and Belles Lettres* in 1820 inaugurated the trend of making Puritanism a dominant theme in the writing of historical romances. Following the republication of Robert Calef's *More Wonders of the Invisible World* in 1823, there appeared James McHenry's *The Spectre in the Forest* in the same year, and the anonymous *The Witch of New England: A Romance* in 1824. Other notable works on different aspects of Puritan history written by the romancers in the 1820s were Catherine Maria Sedgwick's *A New England Tale* and *Hope Leslie*, Lydia Maria Child's *Hobomok*, and James Fenimore Cooper's *The Wept of Wish-ton-Wish*.[8] It should not be surprising that all of this new found curiosity about colonial Puritanism, coupled with the Calvinist-Unitarian contest to wear the modern Puritan mantle, convinced at least New Englanders of the Puritan tradition's past and present reality.

The mood of the romantic period confirmed the reality of the Puritan tradition not only by its interest in the past but in other ways as well. Puritanism was, paradoxically, both an affront and a stimulus to the romantic spirit. The dogmatic aspects of Puritan religion appalled, and even contributed to, the rebellion of nineteenth-century American romantics, notably the Transcendentalists. But other aspects of Puritanism provided

York: Oxford Univ. Press, 1976), especially 350–52, and Perry Miller, *The Life of the Mind in America* (New York: Harcourt, Brace and World, Inc., Harvest Book, 1965), Book One.

[7] Pershing Vartanian, "The Puritan as a Symbol in American Thought: A Study of the New England Societies, 1820–1910" (unpublished Ph.D. dissertation, University of Michigan, 1970), 2–28.

[8] Adelheid Staehelin-Wackernagel, *The Puritan Settler in the American Novel Before the Civil War* (Bern, Switzerland: Francke Verlag Bein, 1961), 39. Staehelin-Wackernagel maintains that whereas American historians took a favorable view of Puritanism throughout the antebellum period, imaginative writers questioned the shibboleths about Puritan piety and virtue from the very beginning of the romantic period.

the romantic with a kind of spiritual ballast for weathering the storms of
the era's radical self-examination of both the individual and the nation.
Furthermore, both Puritanism and romanticism dealt in the language of
absolute truth, inspiring romantics to examine seriously those truths that
to Americans seemed distinctly Puritan.

The core of those truths, and what gradually characterized the independence of Puritanism from Calvinism, was what Santayana, in *The
Last Puritan*, called a "passion for reality," where reality means creation
redeemed and perfected, and passion means a longing so strong it
demands action.[9] Put differently, in the nineteenth century Puritanism
tried to occupy the plane where philosophy of history and ethics inter-
sect in the modern world; but the farther away in time and spirit it
moved from its roots in Calvinism—from the recognition that, as Karl
Löwith has put it, "philosophy of history is . . . entirely dependent on
theology of history"—the weaker its force became.[10] Ironically, only the
critics and not the admirers of Puritanism generally understood this—
understood, that is, that the Puritan tradition was the expression of a
passion for reality made truly luminous only by some transcendent perspective. The defenders and the promoters of the Puritan tradition, once
their faith in the ultimate wisdom and benevolence of God's Providence
was shaken by a process described in Chapter 1, tended to substitute
realities of their own making for that illumined by the faith of the ages.
And as if compensating for the shrinking of the reality for which they
longed, they intensified the passion with which they longed for it,
largely retracing the steps Calvinism took, beginning a century earlier,
from piety to moralism. But whereas Calvinist moralism at least kept
God as its referent, Puritan moralism, while not having exactly the provincial referent H. L. Mencken insisted during the 1920s, lost the distinction between longing and the longed for, finally mistaking heightened
conscience in the individual and in the mass, for creation redeemed and
perfected. As an end in itself, such moralism could survive neither the
ethical relativism nor the excesses committed in the name of morality
characteristic of our century since World War I. And it certainly could
no longer be considered among the noblest things.

Following the description of weakening faith in the ultimate wisdom
and benevolence of God's Providence in Chapter 1, Chapters 2 and 3
review how American historical thought and ethical thought, respectively,
worked to replace providential theology with a Puritan ideology before the
Civil War. Chapters 4 and 5 then analyze two contemporary critiques of
this Puritan ideology, one on the grounds that it was politically corrupt, the

[9] Santayana, *The Last Puritan*, 7.
[10] Karl Löwith, *Meaning in History* (Chicago: Univ. of Chicago Press, Phoenix Books,
1949), 1.

other on the grounds that it was religiously and theologically corrupt. Chapter 6 traces the origin of the genteel tradition in the attempt to rehabilitate the Puritan tradition after the Civil War years exhausted Puritan ideology. Chapters 7 and 8 look at the historical and ethical critiques inspired by this new conception of Puritanism, focused more narrowly now on the anachronism of Puritan elitism and the antisocial ethic of the American Puritan artist. Chapter 9 attempts to explain the background of the Lost Generation's obsession with Puritanism in terms of a final effort to reunite American ideals and American history, and Chapter 10 argues that the equation of the Puritan vision with modern mass democracy during World War I finally sacrificed whatever spiritual authority Puritanism still had to pass judgment on an imperfect world.

Throughout this study claims are made about what different groups of American thinkers contributed to this process of remaking and unmaking the Puritan tradition. It is awkward to qualify each claim by such phrases as "those antebellum Catholics who concerned themselves with Puritanism," but I have tried to do so often enough to remind the reader that this study is based on what the relatively few Americans who participated in the development of the Puritan tradition, even within these groups, said about Puritanism and why. This selectivity posed a problem affecting the method of presentation as well as the syntax. The work is the story of intellectual America's failure to retain Puritanism as a usable past. Thus on the surface the passing of the Puritan tradition appears to be the result of the critics of Puritanism eventually wearing down its defenders and promoters.

At another level, of course, one that provides the background rather than the foreground of this study, the Puritan tradition became unusable because fewer and fewer Americans found its vision interesting or relevant to the rapid changes occurring in their lives. These two levels merge, on the one hand, where the intellectuals attacking Puritanism articulate the grounds of disinterest and irrelevance, but also on the other, where those promoting Puritanism fail to articulate how Puritanism might illuminate the meaning or even the meaninglessness of those overwhelming changes. The bulk of the book implicitly addresses the convergence of elite and mass disenchantment with Puritanism. The conclusion, however, emphasizes the elite's failure to reconstruct the Puritan tradition, not because of any nostalgia for the Puritan legacy, but because of my underlying interest in the process of secularization that this failure represents.

1

The Unjoyous Belief in Providence

Not long before his death in 1860, Theodore Parker, the liberal Unitarian minister, complained in a sermon entitled "Of Conscious Religion as a Source of Joy" that "the unjoyous characteristics of Puritanism still cling to us, and color our mode of religion at this day, and, in spite of ourselves, taint our general philosophy of life." Puritanism was unjoyous, according to Parker, because it was unnatural, and it was unnatural because it discouraged human beings from exercising all of their God-given faculties. To rid itself of this debilitating obstacle to religious joy, Parker advised his generation: "You need the exercise," most especially, "of the moral faculty. This religion will bid you trust your own conscience, never to fear to ask thereof for the everlasting right, and be faithful thereto." Parker's generation was afraid to trust its conscience because it was not certain what "everlasting right" was. In the face of such doubt Parker chided: "Justice will not hurt you, nor offend God." And as evidence of his faith that human beings had nothing to fear by pursuing what they believed justice to be, Parker considered the dangers of harkening to conscience and concluded: "Let me look on all these things, still I am not dismayed. I know, I feel, I am sure of this, that the Infinite God has known it all; provided for it all; that He is all-powerful, all-wise, all-just, all-loving, and all-holy too; no absolute evil shall ever come to any child of his, erring, or sinned against."[1]

In this sermon, Parker considered Puritanism in terms that were much more familiar to his contemporaries than they are to us today. The unjoyous Puritanism he condemned was not, as we might expect, that part of orthodox Calvinism that dwelled on man's condition of sin and natural depravity. Calvinism, by 1860, had already suffered serious, even irreversible, damage at the hands of a generation of liberal Protestant divines in New England. Coupled with the spread of Methodism on the frontier, Calvinism expressed the theological convictions of a majority of American religionists probably only in the South. Puritanism, distinguished from Calvinism, retained something of Calvinism's somber

---

[1] Theodore Parker, "Of Conscious Religion as a Source of Joy," in *Ten Sermons of Religion*, 2nd ed. (Boston: Little, Brown, 1855), 259–60, 291, 304.

mood; but as used by Parker and others of his generation, it referred more generally to the residual sense of human finiteness, contrasted with God's unspeakable sovereignty. Whereas Calvinism had called attention to the consignment of the vast majority of people to an afterlife of everlasting hell, Puritanism centered on the interaction of human activity and divine will in history.

Pressure to abandon Calvinism's conviction that only a chosen few would achieve salvation, no matter how strenuously the many sought redemption, was not a surprising effect of the general democratization of American life in the early decades of the nineteenth century. Protestant theology in the era of the common man, and of the denominational competition accompanying the disestablishment of state churches in the former colonies, found little enthusiasm for the elitest doctrine of the salvation of the elect. Another product of republican egalitarianism was pressure to modify Puritanism's austere rendering of fallen man's confrontation with the inscrutability of God's Providence. If the majority of Americans could now hope to achieve eternal salvation, whether through their own efforts or from God's universal dispensation of grace, then perhaps they could also achieve historical effectiveness. Encouraging belief in the historical efficacy of the masses was the romantic idea of moral progress, born in Europe and domesticated in the United States by many of the same thinkers who were discarding Calvinist elitism.

The struggle between the traditional Puritan belief that Providence governs human affairs in ways not always clear to the human mind nor just to the human conscience and the modern romantic belief that the race not only experiences but can create progress was bitter and protracted, especially in New England. Antebellum Americans perceived the inscrutability of Providence at so many levels of their personal and collective lives, it is hardly any wonder that Theodore Parker found the unjoyous characteristics of Puritanism still so pervasive as late as 1860. At the most spiritual level, Providence and God's sovereignty were synonymous and the appropriate human response was simple submission. Psychologically and philosophically, Providence was fate and the response most often was some rationalization of the apparent impotence of human will. In relation to the development of the nation, Providence was judge and the response was an attempt to reconcile historical and transcendental notions of justice.

Unable to live with the growing problems of immigration, labor conflicts, and above all slavery, many antebellum Americans outside the South eventually abandoned these various expressions of Puritan piety. Abjuring the moral paralysis that the pious submission to the inscrutability of Providence threatened increasingly to produce, they formulated an ideology uniting the romantic promise of moral progress with another Puritan tradition, political activism. This new ideology, defended by

some, condemned by others as seventeenth-century Puritanism transformed, coupled a vision of America's historical mission with the ethical
mandate to, in Theodore Parker's words, "pull down the old kingdom
with its statutes of selfishness and laws of sin and death" and to "build up
a new and better state in its stead, the Commonwealth of Righteousness,
where the eternal laws of God are re-enacted into the codes of man, laws
of love and life."[2] By the Civil War this ideology, more than the
unjoyous belief in the inscrutability of God's Providence, was the essence
of the Puritan tradition that later generations would study, argue about,
and revise again.

The Inscrutability of Providence and Pious Submission

Theodore Parker believed that unjoyous religion was actually irreligion because it was governed by fear. In its "superstitious" form, people
practiced irreligion by trembling at the very mention of God's name.[3]
This was precisely, however, the spiritual attitude many Americans had
long admired in the nation's Puritan fathers and still believed should be
adopted by the pious. The historians George Bancroft and John Gorham
Palfrey recorded the dependence of the Pilgrims and Puritans on divine
Providence as they recorded any other historical fact. Among the Puritan leaders, and especially in times of crisis such as the Pequot War,
"trust in Providence kept guard against despair" and made possible the
virtues of stoicism and perseverance.[4] Among lesser Puritans and in less
strenuous times pious submission to God inspired, according to the Congregational minister George Cheever, other of the "loftiest Christian
graces and virtues" such as faith, hope, and love.[5] Southerners were no
less mindful of the Puritan example than New Englanders, although
they often contrasted the quiet practice of the "doctrine of the meek and
merciful Redeemer" by the Pilgrims with the harder mien of the
founders of Massachusetts Bay.[6] Yet as late as 1845, the *Southern Quarterly Review* commended Puritan piety as the source of "uncomplaining
endurance of the severest toils, patience under various hardships, courage amid appalling perils of all kinds, bravery in battle, and a sturdy

[2] *Ibid.*, 291. For an overview of the providential theme in American history see Robert
P. Hay, "Providence and the American Past," *Indiana Magazine of History* 65 (June
1969): 79–101.

[3] *Ibid.*, 302

[4] George Bancroft, *The History of the United States*, Author's Last Revision, 6 vols.
(New York: D. Appleton, 1924) I: 240; John Gorham Palfrey, *The History of New England*, 5 vols. (Boston: Little, Brown, 1858) I: 468.

[5] George Cheever, "The Inheritance of Principles, Character, and Power Received from
our Pilgrim and Puritan Ancestors, and the Only Means of Perpetuating It" (New York:
John Wiley, 1851), 3–4.

[6] "Political Religionism," *Southern Literary Messenger* 4 (September 1838): 548.

love of independence."[7]

Perhaps with an eye to the heuristic value of the Puritan example, some antebellum admirers of Puritanism were not content simply to record Puritan piety but were anxious to explain it. Harriet Beecher Stowe gave special meaning to the Puritan love of independence by placing it in a dialectical relationship to complete dependence on God. The absence in the New World wilderness of such traditional objects of "deep reverence and profound loyalty" as church, crown, and class, enabled the Puritans, according to Stowe, to submit to God "as King and Ruler . . . without condition, without limit."[8] Unconditional submission to God, in turn, made submission to any other authority intolerable. Commentators less sympathetic to Puritan piety than Stowe explained submission to God by the Puritans' "desperate situation" in the wilderness and need for consolation.[9] But even these accounts constructed a sturdy bridge between colonial and antebellum piety.

Antebellum writers often wrote in praise of their own pious contemporaries in the same terms in which they praised their Puritan ancestors. Uncomplaining performance of public duty and attention to the development of private virtue, when done for the glorification of God rather than for the glorification of self, were no less laudable spiritual qualities during the romantic than during the colonial period. Yet the age of romanticism, with its longing for personal fulfillment and perfection, did present special temptations to place the self ahead of God. The following characterization of William Cullen Bryant's poetry indirectly suggests these temptations. The *Democratic Review* praised Bryant's verses because they displayed "no agonies of passion, no mawkish sensitiveness, no morbid misanthropy, no repulsive egotism, no dragging of private life into public gaze, no unhealthy yearning for sympathy, no childish complaints of the neglect of the world, or of the cruel severities of Providence," all presumably romantic vices. Instead, Bryant proclaimed that "the unceasing vicissitudes of all eternal things indicate the kind hand of Providence conducting the human race through successive trials to the scenes of its noblest triumphs."[10]

Much of the piety of the romantic period was less forbearing than Bryant's, however. Less inspired by willing submission to a Providence deemed kind than by anxiety about life's successive private, economic

---

[7] Review of Thomas Coit's *Puritanism*, in *Southern Quarterly Review* 8 (October 1845): 520–21.

[8] Harriet Beecher Stowe, "New England Ministers," *Atlantic Monthly* 1 (February 1858): 491.

[9] Review of James Savage's edition of John Winthrop's *The History of New England from 1630 to 1649*, in *North American Review* 24 (January 1827): 28.

[10] Review of 5th edition of Bryant's *Poems*, in *Democratic Review* 6 (October 1839): 281–82.

and political trials, it came more to resemble a faith fostered by desolation. In his 1843 articles on "New England Supernaturalism," John Greenleaf Whittier exposed the current obsession with prophecies and omens as traces of a "low, deep questioning of the Future—the utterance of strange hopes and fears, from spirits nervously conscious, amidst the hurry and glare of life's daily presentiments, of the growing and deepening shadow of the Eternal and the Infinite."[11] These "Lines" from the Transcendentalist *Dial* capture the mood Whittier discerned:

> We grope in dimness of light, seeing not ourselves
> We sleep, and dreams come to us of something better,
> We wake, and find that our life is not of Truth,
> We strive, and the powers of darkness contend with our hope.[12]

Whittier was somewhat ambiguous about whether the "dark theory of the Invisible World" propounded an evil essence that was distinct from God's Providence, or whether His agency permitted the existence of evil in order to promote a greater good, as the Puritans had held. But Whittier did clearly perceive that the contemporary preoccupation with "evil in the universe of goodness, darkness in the light of Divine intelligence," was also the source of "everything which our forefathers believed of the spiritual world and supernatural agency."[13] For Whittier, and increasingly for others, brooding about, rather than faith in, the inscrutability of Providence, was the true legacy of Puritanism to antebellum American culture.

Brooding about the inscrutability of Providence could lead to rebellion against uncertainty: to, that is, the external piety of the self-righteous and away from the internal piety of the submissive. Warnings of this danger increased during the antebellum period among those who saw that the inwardly pious became outwardly self-righteous when they presumed to have learned the lessons of Providence and to apply them to changing the world. This presumption was dangerous, in the first place, because of the high risk of misinterpreting the providential will. A parable of a hermit's pilgrimage entitled "The Ways of Providence," which appeared in *Harper's* in 1854, noted that outside the life of the individual, and even then to all but a few, the providential will remained a mystery and the search for justice confounding.[14] The presumption was dangerous, in the second place, because in the nature of things man "cannot act on the outer world as on himself" in obedience to

---

[11] John Greenleaf Whittier, "New England Supernaturalism," *DR* 13 (September 1843): 280.

[12] "Lines," *Dial* 2 (July 1841): 136.

[13] Whittier, "New England Supernaturalism," 282.

[14] "The Ways of Providence," *Harper's* 9 (November 1854): 800.

the decrees of Providence.[15] For all his concern with upgrading the quality of human life and promoting the cause of humanity, even the liberal Unitarian William Ellery Channing ultimately believed that the best-intended efforts to reform the world were so beset by obstacles that "a moral Providence, a retribution" would judge them adversely.[16] Mystified by the growing complexity of the antebellum period, Americans who at one time might have been the most pious in their Puritan-like submissiveness to God's will were now among those on the verge of becoming unPuritan-like in their neglect of the obligation to discern that will and to obey it.

The Inscrutability of Providence and the Problem of Individual Will

As is well known, the great thinkers and writers of antebellum New England had as one of their major themes the spiritual crisis bred by the residue of unjoyous Puritanism. Especially from the publication of Herman Melville's Mardi in 1849 to that of Ralph Waldo Emerson's Conduct of Life in 1860, the psychological and philosophical problems associated with the traditional Puritan tension between individual free will and providential fate received fresh treatment. Making the treatment fresh was the growing sensitivity to the romantic glorification of individualism, perfectability, and progress. But for the most part, northern antebellum writing was not sensitive enough to the culture's urge to escape moral paralysis to embrace romantic optimism without qualification. Although much admired later for their portrayal of the Puritan soul in its final hours of struggle against modernity, the North's most serious antebellum thinkers and writers were not well received in their own day. A sampling of this reception, even more than the works themselves, reveals the emerging rebellion against the paralysis of conscience eventually leading to the formulation of a new activist Puritan ideology.

Commenting on the publication of Mardi, the Democratic Review objected to the Calvinistic portrayal of life in terms of endless cycles of tests of man's obedience to God as well as to the absence of faith in the progressive improvement of mankind: "With all his humanity, Mr. Melville seems to lack the absolute faith that God had a purpose in creating the world. He seems to think that the race is in a vicious circle, from which it cannot escape—that what has been must be forever." Melville put his characters through "baptisms of fire" in which Providence tested their capacity to do good, but the journal saw such trials as pointless because they served no universal goal: "Wherefore these baptisms by fire, if they purify us not," the review asked, "and wherefore is

---

[15] "Success in Life," Harper's 14 (January 1857): 270.

[16] William Ellery Channing, "On the Elevation of the Laboring Portion of Society," DR 7 (July 1840): 63.

one made strong and washed white, if not for others—for all? and can nay *one* be holy and happy until all are?"[17]

In *Mardi*, Melville sends the narrator, mistaken by South Sea natives as the demigod Taji, on a voyage of the world of the mind in a determined search for truth. The "baptisms of fire," which the *Democratic Review* interpreted—characteristically for the times—in moral terms, were, to Melville, struggles to find absolute Truth in partial truths. At the end of the voyage, Melville leaves Taji irresolute, however, about whether human beings are destined to know the whole Truth about the universe. The inscrutability of the search for suprahuman knowledge and wisdom in *Mardi* becomes the inscrutability of the search for divine justice in *Moby-Dick*, published in 1851. Here the monomaniacal Captain Ahab leads a relentless pursuit of the embodiment of evil, the White Whale. During his quest to destroy evil, Ahab goes mad and in the end is killed, along with most of the rest of his crew, by the whale. The only survivor is Ishmael who, as narrator, speaks for Melville. Rather than suspending judgment about the scrutability or inscrutability of the universe, however, Ishmael is able to transcend the antinomies that have made the universe seem so mysterious. He sees "chance, free will, and necessity" as "no wise incompatible—all interweavingly working together." But then, as if taking away with one hand the consolation just extended with the other, Ishmael adds that "chance, though restrained in its play within the right lines of necessity, and sideways in its motions directed by free will, though thus prescribed to by both, chance by turns rules either, and has the last featuring blow in events."[18] Ishmael thus achieves a degree of pious submissiveness to the universe, a submissiveness that might have been admired by Americans in 1831. But his conclusion lacked the moral clarity so much needed in 1851 and, as a consequence, *Moby-Dick* was received no better than *Mardi*.

Nathaniel Hawthorne's *The Scarlet Letter*, published in 1850, and *The House of the Seven Gables*, published the same year as *Moby-Dick*, also failed to meet the public's growing need for confirmation of the existence of moral law and the possibility of moral progress. Because the atmosphere was so heavily Puritan in both works, Hawthorne, more than Melville, seemed at the time to confirm the identification of moral paralysis with the unjoyous philosophy of Puritanism from which his generation increasingly sought relief. Both works portrayed a seemingly or at best partially inescapable burden of sin and guilt: in *The Scarlet Letter*, the immediate and personal burdens of Hester Prynne, her lover Arthur Dimmesdale, and her husband Roger Chillingworth; in *The House of*

---

17 "Melville's *Mardi*," *DR* 25 (July 1849): 50.
18 Herman Melville, *Mardi* (New Haven, Conn.: Yale Univ. Press, 1973); *Moby-Dick* (New York: New American Library, Signet Classic, 1961), 214.

the Seven Gables, the ancestral burden of guilt borne by the Pyncheon family for the colonial hanging of Matthew Maule as an alleged witch.[19] The *North American Review*'s reaction to Arthur Dimmesdale's death on the scaffold, like the *Democratic Review*'s reaction to Taji's "baptisms of fire," indicates that Americans were trying to move away from a world governed by cycles of sin, guilt, suffering, and repentance. The *North American Review* found in these last words uttered by Dimmesdale to Hester the triumph not of the "saintly" phase of his character, which the journal admitted was Hawthorne's intention, but of the "satanic":[20]

> God knows; and he is merciful! He hath proved his mercy, most of all, in my afflictions. By giving me this burning torture to bear upon my breast! By sending yonder dark and terrible old man [Chillingworth] to keep the torture always at red-heat! By bringing me hither, to die this death of triumphant ignominy before the people! Had either of these agonies been wanting, I had been lost forever! Praised be his name! His will be done! Farewell![21]

That Dimmesdale's extreme sufferings could actually point the way to grace and salvation had come to be as morally and psychologically inscrutable to Hawthorne's contemporaries as Taji's inconclusive search for absolute truth or Ishmael's capitulation to mere chance.

Ralph Waldo Emerson, much more than either Melville or Hawthorne, spoke for the romantic generation's need to expose and, where possible, to defy the ancestral conflict between individual free will and providential fate. In his essay in *Representative Men*, entitled "Montaigne, the Skeptic," Emerson witnessed to the pain of realizing that the charity of Providence "is not our charity":[22]

> Things seem to say one thing, and say the reverse. The appearance is immoral, the result moral. Things seem to tend downward, to justify despondency, to promote rogues, defeat the just; and by knaves as by martyrs the just cause is carried forward. Although knaves win in every political struggle, although society seems to be delivered over from the hands of one set of criminals, as fast as the government is changed, and the march of civilization is a train of felonies,—yet general ends are somehow answered.[23]

Emerson referred to these general ends as "destiny" and admitted that

---

[19] Nathaniel Hawthorne, *The Scarlet Letter* (New York: Heritage Press, 1935); *The House of the Seven Gables* (New York: Dutton, 1962).

[20] Review of Nathaniel Hawthorne's *The Scarlet Letter*, in *NAR* 71 (July 1850): 141–42.

[21] Hawthorne, *The Scarlet Letter*, 273.

[22] Ralph Waldo Emerson, "The Young American," *Nature, Addresses, and Lectures*, in *Collected Works*, 8 vols. (Boston: Houghton, Mifflin, 1855) I: 353.

[23] Ralph Waldo Emerson, "Montaigne, The Skeptic," *Representative Men, ibid.*, IV: 185–86.

the destiny of man could never be "discovered in calculated and voluntary activity, but in what befalls with or without [human] design."[24] He did not, however, dismiss people's horror that "the march of civilization is a train of felonies"; nor did he deny that human beings need to feel a part of their destiny. Having wrestled with these questions for much of his life, Emerson presented Americans with a psychology for dealing with the inscrutability of providential destiny in his essay "Fate," published in *The Conduct of Life*.

In "Fate," Emerson internalized the universal struggle between good and evil as a battle of the self against its own limitations. Man was to overcome his bitterness about his own suffering by accepting the consolation of the "double consciousness" that loosened the "old knots of fate, freedom, and foreknowledge" by teaching him that his individual ruin benefits the universe.[25] How different from Ahab's reckless defiance and Dimmesdale's repentance! Furthermore, man was to accept the destiny of the race, to which his ruin made at best a minor contribution, by willing all of the unknown facts and causes that pervert the original intention of freely willed action: "He who sees through the design, presides over it, and must will that which must be."[26] For Emerson, then, the ultimate test of human freedom was its capacity to deny that Providence is inscrutable, that there is any real conflict between free will and fate.

Providential Theory Confronts the Spirit of Progress

The cultural milieu in which Emerson wrote "Fate" was charged with philosophical as well as psychological speculations, especially speculations about the philosophy of history, which Emerson's attempt to psychologize away the inscrutability of Providence could not satisfy.[27] Only at the level of philosophy of history could thinkers more systematic than Emerson try to find an intelligible place for both free will and fate in the providential order, although they too found the reconciliation as difficult as it was necessary. In "Remarks on Universal History," published in the *Democratic Review* in 1843, Orestes Brownson tried to show how the Transcendentalist movement, embodied in Emerson, denied the relative impotence of human will by confusing the traditional

24 Emerson, "The Young American," 351.
25 Ralph Waldo Emerson, "Fate," *The Conduct of Life, ibid.*, VI: 47.
26 *Ibid.*, 27. Stephen E. Whicher's *Freedom and Fate: An Inner Life of Ralph Waldo Emerson* (New York: A. S. Barnes, 1953) presents a compelling analysis of Emerson's struggle with these ideas.
27 Robert Emerson Ireland, "The Concept of Providence in the Thought of William Ellery Channing, Ralph Waldo Emerson, Theodore Parker, and Orestes A. Brownson: A Study in Mid-Nineteenth Century Intellectual History" (unpublished Ph.D. diss., University of Maine, 1972).

notion of Providence with the modern, romantic faith in progress. According to Brownson, the American Transcendentalists compromised the idea of Providence on behalf of a pantheistic theory of development that assumed that man naturally aspires, and because he aspires, he is progressive. By identifying the working of Providence with the "fixed, permanent and necessary law of humanity" that man aspires, the Transcendentalists cast "a doubt . . . on the reality of providential intervention," essential to the traditional understanding of Providence. They implied that God only acts as creator, that "he has in creating man given him all that he ever gives him, made in the very element of his nature all provision for his whole life, here or hereafter, that man needs, or that he does or will make for him." But Brownson objected that "this is precisely what we understand, not by Providence, but by the denial of Providence." Religious orthodoxy had always meant by Providence "a free, sovereign power, distinct from humanity, graciously supplying her from time to time with new strength and materials to work with."[28]

The Transcendentalists were ahead of their time in conflating the ideas of Providence and progress, although Theodore Parker made the "pantheistic providential view of history" the core of the theological liberalism that dominated northern American Protestantism by the Civil War. As late as 1859, however, the *North American Review* presented as orthodox a statement of the traditional providential view of history as made in the nineteenth century, or in the seventeenth century for that matter:

> It is an inexorable law of Providence, that every man becomes in the hands of God the instrument of the rewards and punishments with which he is visited. It is just the same with a people. Nations, except sometimes for a short period, are governed as they deserve. History, then, is not to be judged by the ideal standards of the mind, but accepted as a drama of conmingled human passions, wherein, from scene to scene, from act to act, appear the decisions of Eternal Justice in regard to the *moral* quality of man's deeds.[29]

The emphasis on human acceptance of divine decisions about earthly reward and punishment effectively communicated an attitude of resignation that was as orthodox as the notion of Providence as judge in history. In contrast to romantic philosophies of history that confidently proclaimed the end toward which providential judgment directed events, the orthodox view simply offered a way of understanding particular episodes in the past.

In this respect, one rendering of the idea of progress was compatible

---

[28] Orestes Brownson, "Remarks on Universal History," DR 12 (June 1843): 584, 569, 573, 569.

[29] "Law of Political Development in Civil History," NAR 88 (April 1859): 428.

with the traditional faith in Providence: the law of progress was merely a description of events already observed rather than the eternal *modus operandi* of Providence. Observation of the past indicated that the law of progress actually obeyed a moral law higher than itself. In the short term, Providence withheld the reward of progress when human beings failed to conform their wills to God's. According to the Unitarian minister and Transcendentalist Frederic Hedge, "All progress is judgment. Every generation is a new verdict on human affairs, and the world's history is the world's tribunal. But the progress of society is never a wholly unanimous movement; its judgment is never a unanimous verdict. . . . All civilization is a conflict of opposite forces."[30] In the long term, it was impossible to predict the improvement of the human condition with certainty because the consequences of men's actions lay beyond their control.[31] The ultimate fate of societies and nations, the ultimate fate of history, depended on Providence alone.

Theodore Parker could not even abide this degree of historical fatalism, however, and articulated instead a philosophy to accompany his theology which he believed reconciled fate and free will, Puritanism and romanticism, piety and an active conscience. To Parker, and to the growing number of his liberal Protestant followers, destiny and Providence were the same. They were both the means and the end of achieving a good and harmonious creation; and the moral individual was both an instrument and an example of this human destiny. Parker liked to remind human beings that what made them unique in God's universe was their consciousness that they were "partial cause and providence of [their] own affairs," they were both engine and engineer.[32] As cause, both God and humanity provided the motive and the materials for progress. As providence, God and humanity supplied the purpose and the means of progress. In exchange for the piety and morality of religious conduct, which individuals owed to God, "Providence is what God owes to man; and man has an unalienable right to the infinite providence of God. No sin ever can alienate and nullify that right."[33] Obedience to God's will gives human beings dignity because they then consciously participate in the unfolding of their own destiny; but even without their consent, they

[30] Quoted in Arthur A. Ekirch, *The Idea of Progress in America* (New York: Peter Smith, 1944), 218–19.

[31] Review of Richard Hildreth's *Theory of Morals*, in *NAR* 60 (April 1845): 402. This analysis qualifies the view that the idea of progress negated faith in Providence. See J. B. Bury, *The Idea of Progress* (New York: Dover Publications, 1932) and George Iggers, "The Idea of Progress: A Critical Reassessment," *American Historical Review* 71 (October 1965): 1–17.

[32] Theodore Parker, "The Law of God and the Statutes of Men," *Additional Speeches and Occasional Sermons*, 2 vols. (Boston: Horace B. Fuller, 1867) I: 185.

[33] Parker, "Some Account of My Ministry," *ibid.*, 308.

necessarily benefit from the benevolence of God in fulfilling a progressive purpose for creation. But, in the final analysis, Parker lacked Emerson's realization that God and human beings often have quite different notions of benevolence; or if he realized it, he tried to transcend it with an optimistic faith, as Emerson tried to sublimate it by his double consciousness. And an optimistic faith is precisely what American culture seemed unable fully to embrace in the decades before the Civil War.

The Ambiguity of Providential Judgment on the Nation

Less intellectually gifted Americans also sought escape from the moral ambiguity of history, as pressure for social reform made more urgent the need to reconcile human and divine notions of Justice. Motivated by patriotism rather than by personal spirituality or by the psychological and philosophical encounter between a residual Puritanism and modern romanticism, Americans outside New England also confronted the inscrutability of Providence. The Providence whose inscrutability they confronted as patriotic citizens was neither primarily sovereign nor fate, but judge, although the lines among these images were certainly blurred. In their earliest antebellum reflections on God as judge of the American nation, they were as conscious of participating in a Puritan tradition as were the admirers of Puritan piety and the heirs of Puritan theology and philosophy. From the panic of 1837, which the *Democratic Review* somewhat lamely tried to explain by observing that "every evil in human life has its moral," through the religious revival of the late 1850s, which directed attention to the existence of evil and the need for reform, society wrestled with the confusing implications of the belief that Providence is judge of history.[34] When the nation split apart in 1861, it was at one level seeking escape from unjoyous Puritanism, the inscrutability of providential judgment now having become no more tolerable than the inscrutability of God's sovereignty or of fate.

On the first national fast day in thirty years, occasioned by the death of President William Henry Harrison in 1841, the Presbyterian clergyman and educator John M. Krebs delivered his sermon "Merciful Rebukes" in the classic style of the Puritan jeremiad. "There is no evading the conclusion," he insisted, "derived from the dispensations of Providence toward us, that *God has a controversy with the nation*, and that he is employing our own wickedness to correct us, and our backslidings to improve us." Krebs defended the idea of God's passing historical judgment on the nation by the logic that, whereas individuals have part of their punishment deferred to the afterlife, "nations must meet

---

[34] "The Moral of the Crisis," *DR* 1 (October 1837): 108.

the vengeance here. Their punishment must be complete; and it is equally inevitable."[35] The Unitarian clergyman Orville Dewey detected divine vengeance in the steamboat accident of 1844 which took the lives of several federal cabinet officials. Without attributing transgressions of God's law to the victims personally, Dewey argued that the separation of church and state recently completed with disestablishment in Massachusetts was based on the arrogant notion that power needed no foundation in morality nor any sanction from divine authority, and consequently had evoked God's wrath.[36] Similarly, Theodore Parker thundered against the greed of those men who embroiled the nation in the immorality of the Mexican War, explaining the suffering it caused as "the price of our shame" for violating God's law that "all men are born equal, each with the same unalienable rights."[37]

Given these and other such circumstances, how were those Americans barely clinging to their ancestral belief in Providence to explain the undeniable fact that the United States, for all its arrogance and greed, enjoyed unprecedented growth and prosperity during the 1840s and 1850s? If prosperity were the providential reward for merit, as the nineteenth century like the seventeenth believed, what could the lessons of Providence teach reformers about eliminating America's sins? One possible conclusion was that if progress meant the triumph of good over evil, as some claimed, Providence obviously did not obey a law higher than progress. In fact, by this standard, providential judgment was less severe than that of progress, which still awaited the abolition of evils such as slavery. In this case, some transcendental conviction of what constituted moral progress would have to provide a clearer lesson of the good than providential judgment. Prosperity also confounded reformers because it often benefited the unscrupulous more than the prudent, enlarging the gap between rich and poor, and suggesting that, contrary to accepted moral theory, Providence educed evil from good! William Ellery Channing testified to the growth of uneasy doubts about the value of providential education when he confessed "it is thought that the institutions of this country give assurance that growing wealth will here equally benefit and carry forward all portions of the community. I hope so, but I am not sure."[38]

In the midst of such doubts, the panic of 1857 must have given reformers some sense of moral satisfaction. And even nonactivists greeted the wave of revivalism that followed in the next years as a

[35] John Krebs, "Merciful Rebukes" (New York: Jonathan Leavitt, 1841), 5–6.

[36] Orville Dewey, "The Appeal of Religion to Men in Power" (New York: C. S. Francis, 1844), 7.

[37] Theodore Parker, "Sermon on War," in *Theodore Parker: American Transcendentalist*, ed. Robert E. Collins (Metuchen, N.J.: Scarecrow Press, 1973), 255.

[38] Channing, "The Elevation of the Laboring Portion of Society," 66.

divine outpouring of illumination in a world seemingly lying in "darkness and wickedness."[39] The urgent need for certainty in the highly charged atmosphere of the 1850s, combined with the failure of Providence to teach morally unambiguous lessons of obedience to God's will, made the revival an excuse for discarding the unjoyous faith in Providence and for adopting the assurance of grace in its place.

Traditionally, Christians have distinguished between the instruments of God's grace and of his Providence. Individuals experience God's grace immediately, and it is always benevolent. Providence, on the other hand, is an impersonal force that gradually fits earthly good and evil into God's universal plan. In 1858, the *Southern Literary Messenger* applied this distinction in describing the current "Great Religious Awakening": "Amidst all the aberrations of man from his true moral orbit, there has yet been preserved among his deepest convictions a sense of his dependence upon a Higher Power, and a belief not only in a providence governing the external world, but also in some sort of divine influence flowing into the soul for its purification and guidance."[40] As early as 1850, however, a northerner, George Cheever, had blurred the distinction by associating national prosperity and greatness with grace rather than with providential pleasure, even implying that dependence on God's grace rather than faith in his Providence had also strengthened the Puritans during the colonial period.[41] By the time of the revival of the 1850s, many more northerners, desperate for relief from the moral tension created by the irreconcilable conflict over slavery, found the basis for their conviction of what constituted moral progress in the transcendental outpouring of divine illumination that quickened their consciences rather than in the providential lessons of history.

How little remained of the belief in Providence as judge can be seen in an editorial entitled "Providence in American History," published by *Harper's* in 1858, as the revival was drawing to a close. Had the article been written two decades earlier it would at least have stood as a monument to the piety of the American people. In the 1850s, however, it merely indicated the solitary and rather bloodless posture the journal assumed toward the growing sectional conflict in America. Admitting evidence of past providential concern for the United States, the editorial cautioned against identifying this sense of Providence "with specific measures of national debate" because that would imply that "men could penetrate beforehand the counsels of the Infinite, and infallibly settle the Divine course of action." Quite the contrary:

How the leaven is to work, how the influence is to be communicated,

---

[39] "Politics and the Church," *Harper's* 8 (May 1854): 836.
[40] "The Great Religious Awakening," *SLM* 27 (August 1858): 146.
[41] Cheever, "The Inheritance . . . ," 8, 26.

the intellect of the masses does not perceive. Nor can our statesmen see the mode in which it is to be done. But the impression is stronger for the obscurity in which it is involved. The very mystery that hangs about it is an intimation of divine origin. If it had been the effect of observation, if it had been deduced from the facts by the process of argument, we should be competent to form an opinion as to the means and methods calculated to accomplish the end. As it is, we are just left to execute our task—to show the utility and excellence of republican institutions—and to abide quietly in the faith that the consequences will be shaped by Providence to suit its benevolent will.[42]

Americans who clearly perceived their task as showing the utility and excellence of republican institutions no longer abided in the providential faith very quietly, however—certainly not now that those institutions were so threatened by slavery and secession. Even more to the point, the benevolence of providential will was precisely what Americans were questioning. Had the good intentions of Webster and Clay and Calhoun enabled the Compromise of 1850 to strengthen the Republic? Could Americans really expect the bloodbath of Kansas and Nebraska to benefit the United States? Even to the editors of *Harper's*, providential judgment provided no clear means or methods of achieving moral progress. To other northerners, providential judgment was morally perverse.

On the eve of the Civil War, belief in the inscrutability of Providence was not so much unjoyous as it was untenable. Also no longer culturally useful was the Puritanism that located belief in the inscrutability of Providence at its core. Between 1830 and 1860 a Puritanism so conceived had enabled many Americans to place themselves in a tradition of religious piety, provided the idiom in which New England intellectuals wrestled with the new romantic enthusiasms, and chastened the federal and northern state governments against committing injustices. But by 1860 the cry for morality was louder than that for piety, writers who found salvation in humility were less appreciated, and those who tried to interpret God's judgments were increasingly ridiculed. The sense of historical mission and the ethical mandate to bring in the Commonwealth of Righteousness, which emerged in response to the bankruptcy of belief in the inscrutability of Providence, brought joy to only the northern half of the nation at most; but that sense and that mandate did reveal another dimension of America's understanding of Puritanism that neither half could ignore. Religion and philosophy had not been the whole of the Puritan impulse in the past nor would it be in the nineteenth century. The inability to make an inscrutable Providence help Americans cope with the pressures of change liberated the Puritan tradition to provide instead the vision to give shape to change, to exercise the moral faculty.

---

[42] "Providence in American History," *Harper's* 17 (October 1858): 695.

2

The Seed of Civil Liberty

In order for a new Puritan ideology to emerge, it was necessary, but not sufficient, for belief in an inscrutable Providence to be abandoned. Just as important was for the heritage of Puritan political aspiration, coupled with what Ralph Barton Perry has called "moral athleticism," to be revived.[1] It is doubtful that the historians who so carefully and amply reconstructed the Puritan tradition during the antebellum period were conscious of creating an essential ideological weapon until, perhaps, the eve of the Civil War, although the popularizers of their interpretations certainly were. In any case, the Puritanism portrayed by romantic students of history provided precisely the historical insight a troubled generation could no longer find in the spiritual, philosophical, or patriotic discernment of providential design.

The search for historical insight received its initial impetus and meaning around 1830 not so much from the religious environment transforming the influence of both Calvinism and Puritanism as from the aftermath of the French Revolution. It was in this context that the political theorist George Sidney Camp observed in *Democracy*, published in 1841, that "faith is as necessary to the republican as to the Christian, and the fundamental characteristic of both."[2] He was refuting, on behalf of almost all Americans, the French enlightened assumption that political liberalization depended on secularization, or, in the ideological terms of the day, that republicanism was only compatible with infidelity. For Camp, and many others, American history demonstrated that Christian faith and republicanism were not only compatible but also more productive of human progress than atheism and political liberalization. In the eighteenth century, the American revolutionaries, like the French, may have found it prudent to explain their intention to practice self-government in the secular language of the Enlightenment; but all Americans, eighteenth as well as nineteenth century, knew that the success of their republican experiment depended upon God. Once the horrors of the French Revolution fully exposed the dangers of infidelity, it became

---

[1] Perry, *Puritanism and Democracy*, chap. 10.
[2] George Sydney Camp, *Democracy* (New York: Harper & Bros., 1859), 20.

incumbent upon Americans to demonstrate that Christianity was not only compatible with republicanism but the only sure basis for it.[3]

If Americans were to assert the historical principle that republicanism and Christianity shared the fundamental characteristic of faith, then the Puritan tradition was the logical—indeed, the only—place to begin. Since Daniel Webster delivered his famous Plymouth oration in 1820, New Englanders had argued for the Republic's debt to Puritanism on the grounds that Puritanism was both America's oldest tradition and the only one that linked religious and political reform. With the publication of the first volume of George Bancroft's *History of the United States* in 1834, the Puritan origins of American democracy became a national and not just a regional issue. Puritanism may not have been as liberal as many nineteenth-century democrats would have liked, and they did not hesitate to voice their doubts about the Puritanism-democracy association. But a significant number came to agree that Puritanism did plant the seed of America's political development.

The debate about the Puritan origins of American democracy resulted in different versions of the drama of America's political development. To George Bancroft, writing in the 1830s, Puritanism and republicanism sought to realize a universal law of the spirit. To historical commentators of the 1840s and 1850s the Puritan Commonwealth and the Christian Republic sought to promote what John Winthrop had described in his 1645 speech to the General Court of Massachusetts Bay as the liberty to do good. These variations on the theme of the Republic's debt to Puritanism reflected the growing participation of northern evangelical as well as liberal Protestant reformers in the nation's emerging democratic order. The desire to demonstrate by historical fact that Christianity was the only sure basis for republicanism merged with the need to find in historical theory a morally acceptable vision of America's historical mission. This need, Perry Miller has argued, was also made urgent by the French Revolution.[4] It is ironic, but certainly not without precedent, that such efforts by staunchly Christian Americans to resist the secularizing forces strengthened by the French Revolution actually substantially secularized the nation's religious tradition by weakening its once strong sense of the difference between the divine and the human, the sacred and the profane, the eternal and the historical.

---

[3] May, *Enlightenment in America*, 252–77, 337–57.

[4] Perry Miller discusses the significance of the French Revolution for developments in evangelical religion in *The Life of the Mind in America*, 4–6. On its significance for the development of liberal Protestantism see "Dr. Channing's Recent Writings," *DR* 9 (October 1841): 315–26.

George Bancroft and the Spiritual Bond between Puritanism and Popular Sovereignty

George Bancroft's background was Unitarian and coincided with the early nineteenth-century contest between Calvinists and Unitarians to claim inheritance of the prestigious legacy of Puritan leadership in New England. It inclined Bancroft to find Puritanism beyond the rigid confines of Calvinist theological orthodoxy and especially in the Puritan tradition of civic responsibility. He was also a democrat and the epitome of the romantic student of history, searching for the origins of American society in the patriotic memory of an heroic people who sacrificed everything to realize their most profoundly held beliefs. He was, in other words, representative of his generation's search for an American historical identity that would both confirm and inspire the faith that linked republicanism and Christianity.[5] Thus in volume one of the *History* Bancroft boldly identified Puritanism and democracy on the ground that

> Puritanism exalted the laity. Every individual who had experienced
> the raptures of devotion, every believer, who in moments of ecstasy
> had felt the assurance of the favor of God, was in his own eyes a
> consecrated person, chosen to do the noblest and godliest deeds. . . .
> The issue of Puritanism was popular sovereignty.[6]

Bancroft's association of Puritanism with popular sovereignty did not rest merely on analogy but on three moral principles that he was convinced bound the seventeenth to the nineteenth century: the equation of social and political stability with the fulfillment of universal law; the participation of the common man is that fulfillment; and the unity of Humanity as an expression of God's love. The controversy that the *History* aroused resulted not so much from opposition to these moral principles as from questions of how the Puritan tradition, from colonial to modern times, actually embodied them. Thus Bancroft extended to the national level not only consideration of the Republic's debt to Puritanism but also New England's rivalry among heirs-apparent to the moral authority of Puritanism.

The universal moral law distinguishing Puritan democracy from other kinds of democracy was, according to Bancroft, respect for liberty of conscience. Bancroft did not use liberty of conscience in the individualistic sense of, for example, his contemporary Henry David Thoreau,

[5] In *George Bancroft: Brahmin Rebel* (New York: Knopf, 1944) Russell B. Nye argues that Bancroft was a rebel against the New England tradition. The view taken here is more in line with that of David Noble in *Historians Against History* (Minneapolis: Univ. of Minnesota Press, 1965), chap. 2 and David Levin in *History as Romantic Art* (Stanford, Calif.: Stanford Univ. Press, 1959), 38, which suggest that Bancroft stood more in opposition to the Enlightenment.

[6] Bancroft, *History of the United States*, I: 318.

however. In discussing Roger Williams's banishment from Massachusetts
Bay, Bancroft differentiated between the Transcendentalist-like intellectual freedom asserted by Williams and the civil liberty pursued by such
magistrates as John Winthrop: "High honors are justly awarded to those
who advance the bounds of human knowledge, but a moral principle has
a much wider and nearer influence on human happiness." Winthrop's
defeat of Henry Vane in the election of 1637 during the Anne Hutchinson affair proved, Bancroft believed, that liberty to realize a collective
vision rather than the right to assert private opinions was also the concern of the average Puritan settler: "The contest appeared, therefore, to
the people, not as the struggle for intellectual freedom against the authority of the clergy, but for the liberties of Massachusetts against the
interference of the English government." The democratic creed to which
Bancroft believed Puritanism made a decisive contribution rested on the
priority of a community consensus, attuned to universal and eternal
principles, over individual rights or external demands.[7]

When the third and fourth generation descendants of the Puritans
were on the verge of denying the principle of liberty of conscience, the
theology of Jonathan Edwards appeared, Bancroft contended, to oversee
the transition "from the haughtiness of self-assertion against the pride of
feudalism, to the adoption of love as the benign spirit which was to ani-
mate the teachings in politics and religion." The Edwardsean God, not of
the Enfield sermon, but of *The Nature of True Virtue* and "The Images
of Divine Things" and above all the *History of the Work of Redemption*, became the ground of participation in all aspects of Being, including the pursuit of liberty. All who truly knew and participated in God's
love necessarily promoted liberty because liberty was the principle of
love realized in the life of the community. Those who devoted themselves to the Edwardsean God, Bancroft concluded, led the nation in
winning independence and building the Republic, not because of some
compulsive work ethic, but because "action . . . as flowing from an energetic, right, and lovely will, was the ideal of New England."[8]

Describing the consequences of belief in God as absolute and perfect
right during revolutionary times, Bancroft explained that "the greatest
number in New England held that every volition, even of the humblest
people, is obedient to the fixed law of Providence, and participates in
eternity." He thus reaffirmed the participation of the common people in
fulfillment of the moral law, in addition to equating moral law with
political stability. Not only the leaders of the Revolution but the village
heroes as well "were inspired by the thought that the Providence which
rules the world demanded of them heroic self-denial as the champions of

---

7 *Ibid.*, 255, 259–61.
8 *Ibid.*, II: 405, 407.

humanity." How comforting to Bancroft's age in which the essence of republican virtue was thought to be the ability of the common people to serve the common good! But Bancroft did not only reassure his generation by historical demonstration that, given faith in God, the people would act morally; his special emphasis on the enthusiasm with which lowly seventeenth-century and eighteenth-century Puritans pursued the right facilitated acceptance of the idea that Puritanism could be sympathetic toward a nineteenth-century democracy of feeling.[9]

Nineteenth-century romanticism in general, and its expression in evangelical religion in particular, idealized the common person as an individual who, because he was basically good, could trust the promptings of his heart. The popular Anglo-American image of Puritan New Englanders was, on the other hand, of "a cool, shrewd, calculating, and ingenuous people, of phlegmatic temperament, and perhaps [having] in their composition less of the stuff of which enthusiasts are made, than any other in the world."[10] But Bancroft found in the historical Puritans an energetic passion taking the form of religious enthusiasm in the colonial period and becoming, in the nineteenth century, a moral force that carried the benefits of democratic civilization across the continent. Bancroft's Puritans and their descendants were clearly people of feeling and sentiment, passionately longing to be "morally good and excellent."[11] This transformation in the conception of the Puritans' temperament was one of Bancroft's most important contributions to the equation of Puritanism with democracy.

Bancroft's conviction that the Puritan understanding of the morally good and excellent was eternally and universally true enabled him to overcome scepticism about characteristics associated with Puritanism in addition to its allegedly passionless temper. The Puritan understanding was eternally true, according to Bancroft, because it came from God. It was universally true because human beings were everywhere the same in their ability to perceive this truth, and humanity collectively was heading toward the realization of Truth. Subordination of the individual and even the nation to the Cause of Humanity, the third moral principle that Bancroft believed bound the seventeenth and the nineteenth centuries, thus played a crucial role in Bancroft's perception of the relationship between Puritanism and democracy. In fact, in the last two decades before the Civil War it became the single most important aspect of the issues crystallized in the *History* regarding Puritanism because contemporary events seemed to indicate that the Puritan tradition subordinated

---

[9] *Ibid.*, 407; IV: 157–58.
[10] Quoted from Major Hamilton's *Men and Morals in America*, in *CE* 15 (November 1833): 225.
[11] Bancroft, *History*, II: 407.

the nation and the cause of Humanity to individual conscience.

Bancroft was sensitive to this obstacle to his interpretation, as he had been to the prevailing impression that Puritans were not as passionate as nineteenth-century democrats, and hence he tried to break the connection between Puritanism and belief in the self-importance of the individual. In one of his more reflective passages, he wrote that "the generations of men are not like the leaves on the trees, which fall and renew themselves without melioration or change; individuals disappear like the foliage and the flowers; the existence of our kind is continuous."[12] Yet in his earlier equation of Puritanism with popular sovereignty, Bancroft seemed to place the individual in a one-to-one relationship not only to God but also to the whole of humanity. The idea was rather like Emerson's when he urged in "Self-Reliance": "To believe your own thought, to believe that what is true for you in your private heart is true for all men,—that is genius. Speak your latent conviction, and it shall be universal sense." Emerson later explained that that which was latent in the individual was the all unifying principle of Virtue, "that what is holy is deep." In other words, only the perception of the divine truth uniting all human beings justified the reliance of a single individual on his intuition.[13] Similarly, for Bancroft, the Puritan exalted only that person who experienced the blessing of God and who subsequently devoted himself to obeying God's will, for that individual participated in God's glory which, according to Edwardsean theology, includes "the redemption and glory of humanity."[14]

In "The Office of the People in Art, Government, and Religion," Bancroft drew together the principles on which his equation of Puritanism with democracy in the *History* rested, explaining that government by the people is the strongest government because it rules by moral force:

> The people can DISCERN right. Individuals are but shadows, too often engrossed by the pursuit of shadows; the race is immortal: individuals are of limited sagacity; the common mind is infinite in its experience: individuals are languid and blind; the many are ever wakeful: individuals are corrupt; the race has been redeemed; individuals are time-serving; the masses are fearless: individuals may be false, the masses are ingenuous and sincere: individuals claim the divine sanction of truth for the deceitful conceptions of their own fancies; the Spirit of God breathes through the combined intelligence of the people. Truth is not to be ascertained by the impulses of the

[12] *Ibid.*, 406.

[13] Ralph Waldo Emerson, "Self-Reliance," *Essays*, First Series (New York: Thomas Y. Crowell, 1926), 31, 51, 53.

[14] Bancroft, *History*, II: 406. The foregoing interpretation rejects Russell B. Nye's emphasis on Bancroft's individualism as presented in "The Search for the Individual, 1750–1850," *Centennial Review* 5 (Winter 1961): 9.

individual; it emerges from the contradictions of personal opinions; it raises itself in majestic serenity above the strifes of parties and the conflict of sects; it acknowledges neither the solitary mind, nor the separate faction as oracle; but owns as its only faithful interpreter the dictates of pure reason itself, proclaimed by the general voice of mankind. The decrees of the universal conscience are the nearest approach to the presence of God in the soul of man.[15]

The religious dimensions of Bancroft's faith in government by the people are evident in this passage. Its assumptions are those of a romanticized liberal Christianity akin to Theodore Parker's; but Bancroft had made them consistent with the vision of God transmitted to New England by Jonathan Edwards, who taught that "to love God included love to all that exists; and was therefore, in opposition to selfishness, the sum of all morality, the universal benevolence comprehending all righteousness."[16] Thus Bancroft's identification of Puritanism and democracy in respect for a consensus of consciences, in the affirmation of a passionate and moral human nature, and in the pursuit of the redemption of humanity, allowed both liberal and evangelical Protestantism to embrace the Puritan tradition as the authority for Christianizing America's democratic order.[17]

Liberal Protestantism the True Heir of Puritan Democracy?

The next three chapters examine at some length the historical contribution of nineteenth-century evangelical Protestants and their opponents to the rise and fall of Puritanism as a politically activist ideology. Suffice it to say here that evangelical Protestants welcomed Bancroft's interpretation of the Puritan seed of American democracy without qualification. In advancing their vision of the Christian Republic, they identified themselves with the Puritan tradition explicitly in sermons and Puritan and Pilgrim society addresses, implicitly in their campaigns promoting renunciation of personal vice.[18] Ray Allen Billington described their movement as *The Protestant Crusade* in his 1938 study, subtitled "A Study of the Origins of American Nativism." Despite recent, more sympathetic, accounts of antebellum evangelical reform, the fact remains that in the mid-nineteenth century many Americans, and especially

---

[15] George Bancroft, "The Office of the People in Art, Government, and Religion," reprinted in Nye, *George Bancroft: Brahmin Rebel*, 320–21.

[16] Bancroft, *History*, II: 406.

[17] For general discussions of the Christianization of America's democratic order see, especially, Sydney Ahlstrom, "The Puritan Ethic and the Spirit of American Democracy," in *Calvinism and the Political Order*, ed. George L. Hunt (Philadelphia: Westminster Press, 1965), 87–107; H. Richard Niebuhr, "The Protestant Movement and Democracy in the United States," in *The Shaping of American Religion*, ed. James Ward Smith and A. Leland Jamison (Princeton: Princeton Univ. Press, 1961), 20–71; and Ralph Barton Perry's classic, *Puritanism and Democracy*.

[18] Vartanian, "The Puritan as a Symbol in American Thought," 2–28.

those whose drinking and other personal habits the crusaders tried to reform, believed that the evangelical vision of a Christian Republic was decidedly antidemocratic.[19] Derisively labeling the evangelicals Puritans, these same Americans were, therefore, hardly inclined to equate Puritanism with republicanism. They did, however, accept and even augment the politicization of the Puritan tradition that Bancroft's equation had done much to accomplish by treating the "Puritan" crusaders as political radicals.

The relationship of liberal Protestantism to the identification of Puritanism and democracy was more intellectually fruitful than that of the evangelicals, but like that of the evangelicals, was a reflection of the changing role of liberals, and especially New England Unitarians, in American antebellum democracy. Also like the evangelicals, the liberals' contribution to identifying Puritanism as the seed of civil liberty was as much an effect of their refuting their opponents as of disinterested historical research. Their articulate defense of the continuity between seventeenth-century Puritanism and nineteenth-century republicanism could have, in fact, almost been mistaken for that of the evangelicals by 1860 and indeed was so mistaken by many southerners and midwesterners.

Despite his Unitarian background, George Bancroft was not typical among the New England Unitarians of the 1830s. More theologically liberal, or at least unorthodox than he, they were also more socially and politically conservative. Their claim to have inherited the Puritan legacy of civic responsibility created almost as many sceptics about the compatibility of Puritanism with romantic democracy as did the claim of the evangelicals. By the 1840s, however, forces within Unitarianism promoted the further theological and social liberalization of Protestantism, which they thought would appeal to the romantic, democratic mass. Careful to moderate their style between evangelical Calvinism and conservative Unitarianism, these liberals also carved out a position on the question of Puritanism and democracy between Bancroft's and that of the historian Richard Hildreth, who found no relationship at all between religion and politics in American life. By the 1850s liberal Protestantism defended the same mixed religious and political motives behind colonial Puritanism as behind its own struggle to bring religion to bear on the problems of a democracy threatened with moral subversion by the extension of slavery.

The obstacles the Unitarians, and hence their association of Puritanism and democracy, had to overcome were considerable. Although, as Sydney Ahlstrom has shown, they had adapted the Puritan tradition of

---

[19] Ray Allen Billington, *The Protestant Crusade, 1800–1860* (New York: Macmillan, 1938). See Lois W. Banner, "Religious Benevolence as Social Control: A Critique of an Interpretation," *Journal of American History* 60 (June 1973): 23–41, for an insightful look at the recent literature on antebellum Protestant reform.

civic responsibility admirably in the struggle for independence from Britain, during the first decades of the formation of the Republic they had exchanged their opposition to privilege and corruption for defense of existing authority. Their insistence on obedience to law has come to be regarded as an important Puritan contribution to the political ethos of the United States. But at a time when the content and application of the law was still in its formative stages, it seemed to democrats that conservative Unitarians had used law to combat, rather than promote, the achievement of self-government.[20]

Unitarians also had not always displayed the respect for the masses that defenders of democracy could have expected from the descendants of those Puritans who allegedly founded American republicanism. In 1837, the Unitarian *Christian Examiner* hoped a book by Anthony Grumbler would "counteract in some measure, if possible, the mischievous effects of the gross and extravagant flattery, which, through countless orations, addresses, and newspaper paragraphs, has been hourly administered to the motley multitude called the people of this country."[21] The reviewer feared that the spirit of democracy might be pernicious enough to neutralize the blessings that God had unquestionably bestowed upon the United States. Sharing these reservations about the common people and the ferocity of the levelling spirit in America, the old self-styled Puritan Leonard Withington even criticized that sympathy for the Great Awakening that moved Jonathan Edwards to make "thousands of inferior minds lovers of his abstraction" and recommended instead "a religion which enforces humility."[22]

The final liability Unitarians carried with them to their defense of Puritanism's democratic legacy was the suspicion that the Unitarian-dominated cultural establishment of New England was not providing an adequate foundation for the establishment of a national democratic culture. Contrasting the effect of reverence for intellect in New England with the virtues of a romantic appeal to sentiment, Henry Tuckerman concluded in the *Democratic Review* in 1845 that if Puritan philosophy triumphed in America, the national culture would display a preference for the "mechanical" over the "spiritual" and "mere habit" would usurp the place of "the spontaneous."[23] Praising New Englanders as people of conscience, a *Democratic Review* article on "New Poetry in New England" reiterated the theme that

---

[20] On the Puritan tradition of civic responsibility see Ahlstrom, "The Puritan Ethic and the Spirit of American Democracy."

[21] Review of Anthony Grumbler's *Miscellaneous Thoughts on Men, Manners, and Things*, in *CE* 23 (November 1837): 210–11.

[22] John Oldbug [Leonard Withington], *The Puritan*, 2 vols. (Boston: Perkins & Marvin, 1836) I: 245; II: 265.

[23] Henry Tuckerman, "New England Philosophy," *DR* 16 (January 1845): 85.

they go by foresight more than by hope; what they desire is the reason of the things, and on that they will stand till doomsday or after.
They know most of the force of ideas; in the power of unreflective
enthusiasm, of spontaneous, unquestioning passion, they have less
experience.[24]

This kind of temperament was hardly suited to express the vital currents
in American life in the age of romantic democracy.

Notwithstanding what today would be called their serious credibility
problem, those New Englanders who had inherited the strain of reason in
the Puritan tradition more than the strain of piety would not be denied
their legacy. Several options were open to them for clarifying their position
in the controversy about the Puritan seeds of American democracy. The
most secular and rationalistic might side with Richard Hildreth, who,
apparently oblivious to the excesses of the French Revolution, identified
democratic liberty with "the modern doctrines of religious freedom and
free inquiry." The theocratic idea rather than toleration had inspired the
Puritans, Hildreth insisted, and it began to fade during the Great Awakening when "the revivalists fell back upon the notion of individual salvation . . . leaving politics to worldly men or the providence of God." As a
consequence, Hildreth complacently concluded, "from that day religion
has gone on declining in political and historical importance."[25] Too much
of antebellum life in New England and the rest of the United States still
revolved around finding a way to base the exercise of self-government on
religious and moral principles, however, for Hildreth's view to gain wide
acceptance. A more constructive approach to the controversy was for Unitarians to clarify the relationship between democracy and the Puritan
piety so admired by George Bancroft.

In 1838, as the antebellum Protestant crusade hit full stride, the
progressive Unitarian Orville Dewey distinquished between Calvinist
and liberal piety, warning of the threat the overly pious could pose to
the growth of true democracy. Sensitive to the reputation of New
Englanders as reserved in manners, Dewey blamed not the Unitarians
but the Calvinists, especially the Calvinist clergy's habit of sequestering
itself from all amusements and society, for the "cold, inaccessible, and
repulsive" religion that molded the culture of the region. Favoring a
religion intimately involved with the concerns of everyday life, Dewey
also attacked the social elitism bred by the orthodox Calvinist belief in
divine election:

It is only a false and erring piety, which leads a man to say, "I am
one of the elect of God; I am a favorite of Heaven; and I compare

[24] "New Poetry in New England," DR 20 (May 1847): 392.
[25] Richard Hildreth, The History of the United States, 6 vols. (New York: Harper &
Bros., 1877) II: 390–91.

not myself with the sons of the earth." . . . And it is a false and erring piety, I repeat, which receives earthly discontent and disdain into its bosom, but to lap them in celestial visions, and to buoy them up to dreamy heights of contemplation, above all the rough and staunch conflicts of social life. Many refuges of modern pietism have there been, answering in this respect, the same purpose as the monasteries and hermitages of old.

Finally, Dewey was openly suspicious of the religious enthusiasm that sought to politicize moral issues like temperance. Linking antebellum evangelical reformers with the Puritans not of colonial New England but of the English Civil War, he feared that an army of moral crusaders would subject itself to a "party leader [who] will smile in himself at their zeal, and use their services; and they will find, like the Independents and Roundheads in the time of the second Charles, that they have been deceived and betrayed."[26]

Dewey went so far as to identify the nineteenth-century Calvinist elect with the monastics in the very Roman Church against which conservative Protestants were then beginning to crusade, and to suggest that those seeking to prevent democratic demagoguery might themselves submit to it. Such accusations sufficiently abounded from those outside the internecine struggle for the Puritan inheritance to force liberal Unitarians to remove the controversy about Puritanism and democracy from the ground of contemporary conflict back to that of historical fact. They did so not just to correct the factual distortions that current passions injected into the debate about Puritanism and democracy, but also to advance a particular moral and historical philosophy. Against those, including the transcendental Unitarian George Bancroft, who believed that fate governed the relationship between Puritanism and democracy, other liberal Unitarians began, during the 1840s, to argue that deriving good government from religious principles required conscious action by free individuals, capable of learning and applying the lessons of Providence. Historical judgment of the Puritans must rest, in other words, on the pragmatic issue of how well their government fulfilled their intentions; and the historical relevance of their experiment for the development of a democratic culture, society, and government depended, then, upon how well moderns learned from their mistakes as well as their accomplishments.

Liberal Protestantism and the Political Bond between Puritanism and the Christian Republic

Charles Francis Adams clearly stated the new judgment on Puritan democracy to refute claims made in two controversial 1840 *New York*

---

[26] Orville Dewey, *Moral Views of Commerce, Society and Politics* (New York: David Felt, 1838), 153–54, 197, 184.

Review articles on "The Politics of the Puritans." The articles observed that even though colonial New England charters embodied the principle of popular liberty, Puritan laws abridged some of these liberties, and the extent to which liberty persisted in the colonies was at least in part due to the protection of the kings of England. Adams resented the suggestion that the monarchy had done more for liberty than the Puritans, maintaining "on the Puritans' behalf . . . that out of this unpromising commercial charter which had nothing to recommend it but grant of power, they *by their own act*, for the merits and defects of which they, and they alone, must be held responsible, made a republican form of government." Adams then drew the larger historical and moral implications from these two conflicting views:

> [We] will now take the occasion . . . to enter a general protest against the whole theory of history which has been broached by our author in both of his articles. We regard it as utterly subversive of all right judgment upon human action, as well as of the ordinary and only sound rules of moral discrimination. We shall never assent to the doctrine, that the principles of popular liberty now universally recognized among us to be true, have been the offspring of circumstances only, nor that the most arbitrary monarchs known in history are the most meritous promoters of their spread. We desire to look into the records of the past for the important lessons it can give to mankind for the future. If they have to tell us only of lucky accidents, then let the books be shut up for ever. . . . Men need not trouble their heads with the stream of time, if they have nothing to do but float upon it. . . . The great element for all judgment of actions is the intent.

In other words, whereas the *New York Review* called the Puritans agents of free government in the sense of their being "mere instruments," Adams understood their agency to have been responsible moral action.[27]

Adams's view of history was clearly more generous toward colonial Puritans than that of the *New York Review*, but it created more problems than it solved for those seeking justification and guidance for the Unitarian vision of a Christian democracy. It seemed to ignore the difficulties Americans were having interpreting and applying the lesson of Providence in the middle of the nineteenth century, discussed in chapter 1. And establishing that the fathers of New England intended to institute self-government answered neither toward what end they intended to govern themselves nor whether that end was the same as that envisioned for self-government in the nineteenth century. Critics of Puritanism, past and present, tended to value self-government as an end in itself, especially as Americans grew increasingly unable to agree on any larger purpose the

---

[27] Note on "The Politics of the Puritans," *NAR* 51 (July 1840): 268, 269–71. The *New York Review* article originally appeared in January 1840, to which the *NAR* offered an initial response in "The Politics of the Puritans," 50 (April 1840): 432–61.

United States should serve. As the crucial decade of the 1840s pressed on, liberal Protestant defenders of Puritanism, on the other hand, moved closer to George Bancroft's understanding of democracy as, in Orestes Brownson's words, "Eternal Justice ruling through the people."[28] They agreed, that is, that the Puritans had helped make the will of God, rather than the will of the people, the true end of self-government in the United States. But most significantly, by the 1850s many liberals took one additional step, placing them very close to the evangelicals, in principle at least. They now affirmed that in the seventeenth century, and in the nineteenth as well, a Christian Commonwealth was compatible with a republican or democratic form of government.

In an 1853 comment on Hawthorne's *Blithedale Romance*, the *North American Review* gives us a clue to how liberal thinking might have evolved from crediting colonial Puritanism with planting the seed of American civil liberty to admiring the Puritans' Christian Commonwealth:

> We do not believe that the Creator ever intended that human institutions and arrangements should produce worthy and valuable results independently of individual virtue. It is incident to our probation as moral agents, that the bands, wheels, and pullies of the social machine should be constantly liable to be thrown out of gearing, without weights of our own devising,—without the unintermitted and earnest exercise of the best powers and purest affections. It is a wakeful sense of justice, a religious love, an active humanity, that alone can distribute the gifts of God with equity. The only self-adjusting social system must be that of a thoroughly Christianized commonwealth.[29]

If, as most mid-nineteenth-century Americans wanted to believe, the current institutions and arrangements in the United States were fundamentally committed to moral liberty, then the Puritans must have intentionally and rightly set it up so. To maintain that commitment, Americans had continually to practice the virtues of justice, love, and humanity. To remove some of the uncertainty about how to practice those virtues in support of civil liberty, the Puritans established a commonwealth that translated virtues into political principles. Thus, the thoroughly Christianized commonwealth was Christian in its means as well as its ends. The implication of such an analysis for mid-nineteenth-century Christians would have been clear: go and do likewise.

Liberal Protestant acceptance of some form of John Winthrop's principle that the only liberty worth having is the liberty to do what is good and just, in the end placed liberal Protestantism in a paradoxical relationship to the Puritan tradition. On the one hand, liberal Protestant

---

[28] Orestes Brownson, "Origin and Ground of Government," *DR* 13 (October 1843): 353.
[29] Review of Nathaniel Hawthorne's *The House of the Seven Gables* and *The Blithedale Romance*, in *NAR* 76 (January 1853): 247.

reformers sought to apply the principle of moral liberty by joining reform movements, and especially the antislavery movement, in increasing numbers. But in doing so they risked validating the now oft-heard accusation that political motives had, and always had had, a higher priority in Puritanism than religious motives. On the other hand, however, their recognition that the Puritans sought to establish a Christian Commonwealth, rather than merely a nineteenth-century style republic or democracy, enabled liberal Protestants to resist the total politicization of the meaning of Puritanism. And by the 1850s resistance was necessary. When New England's loyal son John Gorham Palfrey published the first volume of his *History of New England* in 1859, affirming religion as the dominant theme in the Puritan tradition, the *Christian Examiner,* *Harper's*, and the *Atlantic Monthly* had to rally to his defense.[30] After a quarter century of debate about what kind of political order the Puritans instituted in the United States, the dominance of religious concerns in the Puritan tradition was no longer self-evident.

In response to the new nation's need for an historical identity based on the compatibility of Christianity and republicanism, Bancroft's *History* inaugurated a debate that radically politicized the meaning of Puritanism. Why did this politicized Puritanism become the symbol of America's historical identity in the mid-nineteenth century? The most obvious answer is that the Puritan tradition offered the only indigenous alternative to the formal separation of church and state in the United States, which was still beset with unresolved problems.[31] Supporters of separation could blame residual Puritanism for the failure of disestablishment; opponents of separation, closeted as they had to be, could use Puritanism to judge the merits—or to them the demerits—of the success of disestablishment. In any case, the increasingly heavy burden of slavery denied the United States the leisure to wait out the natural adjustment of political morality to religious toleration. Among the most impatient, the historical identity symbolized by Puritanism provided the materials for an activist political ideology. American history as interpreted by the Bancrofts and Adamses highlighted the moral purposefulness shared by the seventeenth-century Puritan Commonwealth and the nineteenth-century Christian Republic. Thus, when philosophical Puritanism became untenable because it instilled moral paralysis, the political history of Puritanism offered both a vision of America's historical mission and a moral imperative to fulfill it.

---

[30] Reviews of John Gorham Palfrey's *History of New England*, in *CE* 66 (January 1859): 137–39; *Atlantic* 3 (April 1859): 442–43, 448–49; and *Harper's* 18 (April 1859): 692.
[31] See John F. Wilson, ed., *Church and State in American History* (Boston: D. C. Heath, 1965).

3
The Puritan Ideology

In the century before romantics like George Bancroft reinterpreted the Puritan tradition, Anglo-American Puritanism had, generally speaking, not been much admired. The prevailing Puritan authorities, the British Tory historians Clarendon and Hume, had portrayed as illiberal excesses the political actions of the English regicides and Commonwealthmen, and the American persecutors of Quakers. The romantic era, on the other hand, in Europe as well as in the United States, viewed Puritan politics either as an unfortunate residue of despotism soon to pass or, more frequently, as a necessary excision of lingering threats to the triumph of a new liberalism. New Englanders embraced the latter interpretation; the rest of the United States adopted either the former or, in much of the South, even the Tory. It followed that Americans who were not descendants of the early Puritans, and whose critiques of Puritanism are the subject of the following two chapters, tended to be as suspicious of nineteenth- as of seventeenth-century political moralism. In contrast, New Englanders tended to treat the redeemed reputation of Puritan reformers as both historical and ethical validation for politicizing nineteenth-century moral issues. In this chapter I will examine the political moralism that, justified by romantic historiography, cemented the formulation of a new Puritan ideology.

Pietism and Puritan Politics

After reading Macaulay's, Carlyle's, and Guizot's revisions of the historiography of Clarendon and Hume in 1846, George Lunt warned readers of the *Christian Examiner* that

> the price we pay for our political and religious privileges is unceasing watchfulness and perpetual revolution. . . . The reformers will not let us rest. . . . But probably it is necessary. It may be the chief condition upon which Providence allows us to retain what we most value. . . . To all who study Providence as unfolded and recorded in history, it cannot but be apparent, that we must either, in our day and generation, do our duty faithfully, and reform abuses gradually, as we discover them, or we must let them grow and multiply a hundred for one, and mercilessly leave to our successors on the stage of life to do battle, (and a bloody battle it must then ultimately be!)

with the monster which a slight effort might have strangled in its
birth.[1]

Implied in the context of this warning is not only the equation of Puritanism with the privileges of republicanism but also an ethical mandate
from the Puritan past either to make politics responsive to religious and
moral values or to expect the demise of republicanism. Lunt, prophetically, alluded to the consequences of ignoring the abuse of slavery, but
his fellow clerics were as likely to be worried about the abuses of drink
and popery as well. The threat perceived by all the moral reformers in
the second quarter of the nineteenth century went far beyond the sug-
gestive but mechanical "self-adjusting social system . . . thrown out of
gearing" feared by the proper *North American Review* in its 1853
review of *Blithedale Romance*. It much more closely resembled the fear
of the coming of the Antichrist, the staple of more emotional, and especially of revivalistic, opinion.[2]

Even though nineteenth-century revivalism came to be dominated
by evangelical groups, such as the Methodists, who explicitly renounced
Calvinist theology, the roots of American revivalism were in the Calvinist tradition. The moral theory of revivalism as well as its techniques
had as their fountainhead the eminent eighteenth-century Calvinist theologian Jonathan Edwards of Massachusetts. Edwards's successors, the
New Divinity men, later abandoned revivalistic practices as unbecoming
the intellectuals they were but perfected Edwardsean moral theory into
a potent weapon in the battle against Antichrist, a drama in which
Edwards himself had believed quite literally. In a later and simplified
form, this revised Calvinist moral theory provided the content of the
ethical mandate that moral reformers believed history, and especially the
romantic version of Puritan history, issued them. By 1852, as liberals and
evangelicals moved closer together in their drive to Christianize the
United States, the Unitarian minister Rufus Stebbins could admit in the
Christian Examiner that since publication of Edwards's *Freedom of the
Will*, in 1754, "New England theology is Calvinism in an improved
form. . . . They saved the old theology from annihilation by maintaining
that all sin to which guilt is attached is actual. 'Sinning is acting' was
their creed." In other words, since the Great Awakening of the 1740s,
American Protestant thought had paid less attention to the abstract point
that original sin was the source of immoral conduct and more to the
practical duty of the regenerate to renounce immorality and strive for

[1] George Lunt, "Oliver Cromwell and Puritanism," *CE* 40 (May 1846): 456–57.
[2] Alice Felt Tyler's *Freedom's Ferment* (Minneapolis: Univ. of Minnesota Press, 1944)
remains the most comprehensive treatment of antebellum reform and Book One of Perry
Miller's *The Life of the Mind in America* best explains the reform movement's religious
origins.

the perfected state of sanctification.[3] Assuming the considerable burden of what sin traditionally connoted in New England, evil deeds came to produce stronger feelings of guilt about individuals' imperfect conduct than the doctrine of original sin had produced about humanity's imperfect condition. And with the proper manipulation by reformers as well as by revivalists, those feelings of guilt were most likely to receive expiation from the exertions of "moral athleticism."

The creed "sinning is acting" readily inspired pietist crusades against such personal vices as the excessive consumption of alcohol. Although often preached to the unregenerate in the hope that reformation of conduct would eliminate sin—that, in traditional Calvinist language, the process of regeneration might be reversed and sanctification precede justification—pietist reform tried even more to organize the already converted to strive for perfection in conformity with uniform rules of moral conduct. As Cushing Strout has convincingly shown in *The New Heavens and New Earth: Political Religion in America*, the origins of the voluntary associations, which initially conducted reform crusades and later put pressure on government to legislate morality, resided in this twofold purpose of converting others away from sinful action and presenting the sinless action of the already regenerate as a model of social organization.[4]

The abolitionist crusade, while sharing the organizational wisdom acquired by the pietists, rested on what can be understood as an additional transformation of the neo-Calvinist doctrine that "sinning is acting." In matters of personal conduct, such as drinking, sinful action was clearly evil, sinless action was clearly virtuous, and no action, had it been possible, would have lacked a moral quality. In the matter of slavery, however, the moral quality of no action was ambiguous. Slaveholding was considered clearly evil and opposition to slavery clearly good, but what about indifference, or at least inaction? As the antislavery movement became more radical, opponents of slavery increasingly insisted, at least implicitly, that sinning was not acting; sinning was, that is, failing to join the antislavery movement or, in the even more sensitive case of the state, to abolish slavery.

The innovation that "sinning is not acting" capitalized on the personal guilt of those who, in their hearts, believed slavery was wrong but did not join the antislavery movement because the law of the land permitted slavery. Doing nothing to remove the evil of slavery, the revised creed taught, was as sinful as the act of enslavement. Furthermore,

---

[3] Rufus Stebbins, "The Andover and Princeton Theologies," *CE* 52 (May 1852): 333. Haroutunian's *Piety versus Moralism* remains the best work on this subject.

[4] Cushing Strout, *The New Heavens and New Earth* (New York: Harper & Row, 1974), chap. 7.

sanctioning, however tacitly, the laws protecting slavery perpetrated the social sin of injustice for which the entire community was responsible. Thus "sinning is not acting" embodied the equation of sin with both individual and collective evil, enabling an abolitionist like George Cheever to impose a double burden of guilt in his 1849 sermon, "The Curse of God Against Political Atheism":

> Every sufferance of such execution, every lending of themselves, either on the part of magistrate or people, as instruments of such wrong in the name of law, and under the pretence of law, is just the deliberate commission of two crimes instead of one. First, it is the transaction of the original crime—injustice, inhumanity—which is a sin against God and man; and second, it is the practice of the crime, in the name of the law, which is an added sin, especially against God, and is the daring assertion that human law is higher than the Divine.

The abolitionists denied that human law is higher than, or even as high as, divine law; and hence, if the two conflict and the higher law is not obeyed, the transgressors "shall be utterly cast out from the kingdom of heaven."[5]

At issue in Cheever's address was the Fugitive Slave Law, a federal statute largely unenforced since its passage in the 1790s but given new authority by the Compromise of 1850. Two months before Cheever delivered "The Curse of God Against Political Atheism," New York's abolitionist Senator William Seward, debating the disposition of territories ceded by Mexico in the recent war, had made the concept of a "higher law" a commonplace in the Compromise debate and the intensified slavery controversy that ensued: "the Constitution devotes the domain to union, to justice, to defence, to welfare, and to liberty. . . . But there is a higher law than the Constitution, which regulates our authority over the domain, and devotes it to the same noble purpose."[6] In doing so, Seward and those abolitionists who invoked the higher law notion over and over again expressed nineteenth-century Puritan ideology in its ultimate form. The politicization of sin implied in the notion of higher law completed the evolution of Edwardsean moral theory to which the romantic interpretation of Puritan history had given such support. Those who were lukewarm in their opposition to slavery not only carried a double burden of guilt for their sinful inaction but were also now labeled criminals by the ideology for transgressing the higher law that was both moral and historical. As the sin of inaction was both personal and communal, the crime of violating the higher law was both

[5] George Cheever, "The Curse of God against Political Atheism" (Boston: Waller, Wise, 1859), 11.

[6] William H. Seward, "California, Union and Freedom" (Washington, D.C.: Buell & Blanchard, 1850), 8.

communal and cosmic, because the United States was involved in the universal struggle between the forces of Christ and Antichrist.[7]

Appeal to a higher law than the Constitution and the fugitive slave statute paradoxically sealed the politicization of the Puritan tradition in mid-nineteenth-century America. It placed otherwise law-abiding citizens on the far side of civil law through acts of civil disobedience and, simultaneously, it stepped up political pressure to repeal those provisions and statutes condoning slavery. The moral convictions of the opponents of slavery were no longer merely private convictions, acted upon through participation in voluntary associations organized to achieve moral progress voluntarily, or, at most, by consensus. They became translated into public actions with consequences not only for the individual moralist but for the political system, constructed as it was to embody compromise among interests rather than the victory of the absolutist conscience. Yet, victory for the absolutist conscience is what the opponents of slavery, popery, drunkenness, and personal vice, in the hothouse political environment of the 1850s, increasingly wanted. Hence, we can speak of the politicization of Puritanism in the years immediately before the Civil War because the ideology justifying the pursuit of political victory for the absolutist conscience derived from the reconstruction of the Puritan tradition. As Puritan spirituality declined, faith in Providence was replaced by faith in progress; but progress was defined in terms bequeathed by Puritanism, either as the spread of a democracy respecting the spiritual autonomy of each individual in the 1830s or, by the 1850s, as the elimination of sinful behavior and institutions. Furthermore, a combination of residual Puritan and romantic enthusiasms gave this ideology its normative power in its identification of moral progress with historical salvation and the elevation of the troubled conscience above existing institutions. That this rendering of traditional strains within Puritanism occurred in a republic, where church and state were formally separated at the state and federal levels, distinguishes the Puritan tradition reconstructed as ideology from the original sixteenth- and seventeenth-century movement. And we might also note that the antebellum Puritan ideology can be distinguished from later pietist efforts merely to legislate morality by the latter's relative neglect of philosophical, historical, and cosmological justifications. That the Puritan ideology retained these intellectual foundations while pietistic moralism did not can be interpreted as a sign of the surprising vitality of the Puritan tradition as late as the Civil War.

In any case, the use of political power to achieve moral ends, when

---

[7] The problem of guilt and abolitionism is treated somewhat differently in Stanley Elkins, *Slavery* (Chicago: Univ. of Chicago Press, 1959) and in Aileen Kraditor, *Means and Ends in American Abolitionism* (New York: Random House [Vintage Books], 1968).

these ends are dictated by a higher law that is not only ethical but also historical, is what an American commentator would most likely have meant by the adjective "Puritan" and the noun "Puritanism" at mid-century. The explicit identification of Puritanism with the legislation of righteousness was largely the work of opponents of politico-moral reform, discussed in the next two chapters, although few politico-moral reformers rejected the label Puritan. Perhaps the fact that most were resident or displaced New Englanders, that most welcomed the historical proof of continuity between Puritanism and republicanism, that most acknowledged the Calvinist roots of their conception of evil, enabled such reformers to wear the Puritan label with pride rather than shame. In any case, they certainly could not deny that their Puritan ancestors became proficient in the use of political means to achieve religious and moral ends or that their own efforts were increasingly similar to those of the Puritans. Modern historians have recognized the origins of nineteenth-century revivalism, millennialism, and perfectionism in the Puritan impulse. Nineteenth-century commentators would have added an additional, and perhaps qualifying, debt: the belief that the state was the proper instrument for promoting moral progress.

Moderation and Puritan Citizenship

The politicization of the Puritan tradition, and particularly the fact that the process reached maturity through defiance of the very fragile Compromise of 1850, troubled many Americans who, unlike those discussed in the next two chapters, also wanted to Christianize the Republic. Like the abolitionists, they wanted to create and preserve a moral society, but these more moderate reformers questioned the abolitionists' methods. They believed, for example, that the abolitionists betrayed their commitment to a moral social order by refusing to accept punishment for the civil crime of disobeying the Fugitive Slave Law. Moderates also believed it was presumptuous and subversive of order to urge, as the abolitionists did, duly constituted public officials not to enforce legal statutes such as the one requiring the return of fugitive slaves, but instead, to uphold moral principles that had not yet found statutory expression. In the long run, such a cavalier attitude toward the law of the land would, the moderates claimed, obfuscate rather than illuminate the problem of how to build a Christian Republic.[8]

Moderate reformers hoped that republican religion, with independent churches educating individuals to govern themselves according to moral law, would provide a better link between Christianity and democracy in the United States than the outright legislation of righteousness.

8 "The Conspiracy of Fanaticism," DR 26 (May 1850): 392.

Republican religion had once been moderate Protestantism's accommodation to the disestablishment of the church, but by the 1850s it seemed that both separation of church and state and republican religion had been severely weakened. Abolitionist pressure on the federal government to prohibit slavery resembled the sectarian behavior of nativists and pietists who urged local governments to legislate against Catholics and personal vice. Having witnessed the politicization of Puritanism, and fearing the same fate for Christianity, in the 1850s moderate reformers mounted an effort to instill republicanism with moral authority by substituting the practice of Puritan citizenship for the practice of Puritan politics. The infusion of Christian piety into all levels of civic life, rather than the manipulation of politics to achieve specific moral ends, would distinguish Puritan citizenship from Puritan politics; and the resulting government would attune itself to the moral order governed by Providence rather than to the dream of moral perfectionism. Puritan ideology would not be abandoned, but it would be modified to respect the principle of religious toleration.[9]

During a decade of thoughtful comment on the participation of the clergy in the politico-moral struggles of the day, *Harper's* magazine most fully articulated the moderate view. The informing spirit behind *Harper's* advocacy of Puritan citizenship was originally the desire to maintain the purity of religion, more than to Christianize the state. The romantic period specifically threatened the purity of religion, according to *Harper's*, by the popularity of the voluntary associations and the decline of theological orthodoxy. When religion politicized and moralized all human problems, politics as well as religion eventually suffered because religion relinquished its proper role as transcendent judge of human action: "religion will cease to be politically *useful* when its political *utility* is presented as the true or pretended ground of its support."[10]

Harper's blamed the voluntary association for the secularization of the clerical ministry in antebellum America:

> Christianity has given birth to a large class of semi-religious institutions, that are working effectually for the improvement of mankind. Indeed, of late years no small degree of its power has appeared in the moralization of society rather than its absolute Christianization. . . . A religious worldliness is easily generated in the midst of these influences, and ere he is aware, the minister of the sanctuary is led into a secular temper of mind.[11]

Harper's worried lest the worldly orientation of the voluntary association

---

9 Strout, *New Heavens and New Earth*, chap. 10, analyzes abolitionism as a sect in much the same way nineteenth-century moderates did.
10 "The Position of the Clergy," *Harper's* 9 (June 1854): 215.
11 "The American Pulpit," *Harper's* 12 (May 1856): 843.

movement make the church subservient to the state. In *The Inner Civil War* George Fredrickson likened *Harper's* advocacy of "theocracy" during the Civil War to that of the liberal Protestant, Horace Bushnell; but evoking an oft-quoted passage from Bushnell's *Barbarism the First Danger* seven years before the war, the journal warned of the pitfalls in Bushnell's vision that "the millennium is to be ushered in by political movements, and be itself a sort of politico-religious golden age. Christianity is to cover the earth with railroads and telegraphs, and these again to diffuse Christianity with a speed unknown to apostolic times." And then it pondered: "Is there not some reason to fear that in such a course, instead of the Church's spiritualizing the world, the world will secularize the Church, or that it will be made as completely subservient as though it had been bound to the State by some direct and clearly-defined connection[?]"[12]

Furthermore, *Harper's* complained, romantic theology had discarded the "graphic language of the Bible" and the "homilies of the Puritan expounders of the five theological points" for the "transcendental euphemism of the Neologists" and moral lectures exploiting the intellectual fad of millennialism.[13] Instead of reminding men that the purpose of government is to serve the will of God and calling attention to the original political sin of self-interestedness, ministers took sides on specific political measures. "If the pulpit of today were baptized by the outpouring of the loving and self-sacrificing spirit of the crucifixion," *Harper's* concluded, "this morbid, restless, turbulent age would find its perfect place in the bosom of God."[14]

John Brown's raid on Harper's Ferry in 1859, like the Fugitive Slave Law almost a decade earlier, gave new urgency to the distinction between Puritan politics and Puritan citizenship. *Harper's* recognized that the spirit of sectarianism, represented by Brown's and his supporters' attempt to impose their own solution to the slavery crisis, owed something to the "intense subjectivity of [Puritan] independency." Instead of renouncing the Puritan tradition altogether, however, the journal asserted that the ideal of the loyal citizen, represented by the Puritan clergy, would triumph over sectarianism and give America a government that enjoyed the blessing of Providence.[15] As a result of the "old Puritan Character . . . the American connects his faith in the divine calling of his country with a just conviction of his personal birthright as a

[12] "The Position of the Clergy," 115. The citation in Bushnell is *Barbarism the First Danger* (New York: William Osborn, 1847), 27. George Fredrickson discusses this question in chap. 9 of *The Inner Civil War* (New York: Harper & Row, 1965).
[13] "The American Pulpit," 845.
[14] *Ibid.*, 844. See also "Pulpits and Preachers," *Harper's* 18 (May 1859): 839–43.
[15] "National Life," *Harper's* 22 (January 1861): 264.

citizen, a Christian, and a man."[16] Therefore, the duty of the American citizen was to support his government, erected on the principles of love for God and for liberty, in the confidence that, under providential guidance, even the persistence of slavery would serve a higher purpose. Other northern journals of opinion later followed *Harper's* in equating the religious duty of loyalty with the "distinctively providential element" in the establishment of government in America and in citing the Puritan minister as the prime example of the good citizen.[17]

When the Civil War came, *Harper's* defended its ideal of Puritan citizenship by linking it with a desire for theocratic government in the United States:

> The more seriously we acknowledge this great fact, that authority comes from God, and that all who bestow or exercise power are bound to act under responsibility to him, we exalt democracy from its too frequent and monstrous man-worship into the realm of divine law, and we count its votes not merely by bodies but by souls, calling no voter a soul who does not own his responsibility under God, and try to do what is right before him, instead of doing merely what is pleasing in his own eyes. . . . So in our way, we accept the *theocratic* idea [emphasis mine], and are ready to say, not that the voice of the people is the voice of God, but that it ought to be His voice . . . the government of the many is respectable only when it freely seeks out the merit of the few, and delights to put the best men into the seats of highest power.[18]

Theocracy meant to the author of this article, entitled "Discipline," not ecclesiastical rule but more what it means to the historian Charles Barker when he describes as theocratic the government of Massachusetts Bay before 1680: "The question of theocracy depends on whether or not visible saints, *God's elect* as surely as the Puritans could tell, had power."[19] In nineteenth-century America the nation's visible saints were, according to *Harper's*, those who, "with prayer and a united waiting on God," upheld the authority of divinely instituted government against those who would use the state to realize their own personal moral visions.[20]

The Politicization of the Puritan Tradition

By casting the crisis of mid-century republicanism in terms of a choice between Puritan politics and Puritan citizenship, *Harper's* crystallized two

---

[16] "Our American Dignity," *Harper's* 22 (December 1860): 118.
[17] See, for example, "Loyalty," *NAR* 94 (January 1862): 161–62, and "Valor," *Harper's* 23 (August 1861): 408–09.
[18] "Discipline," *Harper's* 24 (January 1862): 261.
[19] Charles A. Barker, *American Convictions: Cycles of Public Thought, 1600–1860* (New York: Lippincott, 1970), 69–70, 54a.
[20] "Duties of the Citizen to Civil Government," *Harper's* 20 (April 1860): 698.

important issues surrounding the antebellum reinterpretation of the Puritan tradition in New England. The first was that Puritanism had become politicized. As a philosophical attitude and as history, Puritanism had succumbed to contemporary political pressures to find an ideological rationale for circumventing the constitutional separation of church and state. Like all ideologies, the one now attached to the Puritan tradition retained religious and moral elements and, indeed, gained much of its acceptance from them. But religion and ethics were now placed in the service of radical social change.

The second issue dominating the antebellum reinterpretation of Puritanism was the crisis of leadership in the North. Bancroft's *History* had addressed this issue by validating the moral principle of democratic self-government, but in the thirty years since the publication of the first volume of the *History* the Republic had learned that governing itself according to moral law was an extremely difficult task. The burden of balancing religion and politics in the North had come to rest on competing elites, not on the democratic mass apotheosized by Bancroft; and those elites both sought their authority in the Puritan tradition. Puritan politicians and Puritan citizens viewed themselves to some extent as remnants of a movement born over two centuries earlier to purify human institutions of corruption. The social sins of the masses having proved intractable, morally enlightened leaders had to save the nation from moral degeneration and historical defeat, whether by manipulating or by transforming the state.

Even the editors of *Harper's*, however, were too caught up in responding to the mid-century crisis to see clearly the full consequences and significance of the antebellum politicization of Puritanism. They did not understand that if the triumph of Puritan ideology failed to redeem America, religion and politics, as well as church and state, would come to occupy separate realms; and the nation's democratic experiment would have difficulty claiming the support of religious fidelity. Nor did they fully grasp how much spiritual power the Puritan tradition had already lost to secularization. Only critics of Puritanism perceived the damage done to both republicanism and Christianity by the politicization of the Puritan tradition. Their critiques, along with the morally ambiguous outcome of the Civil War, began to strip Puritanism of the moral authority to define and shape America's historical identity so laboriously reestablished during the antebellum period.

4

"Political Religionism"

The attention lavished by New Englanders on the Puritan tradition during the romantic period created the impression that Americanism was almost synonymous with Puritanism. The practical efforts of New England reformers to model American life and institutions after Puritan principles suggested that if Americanism were not yet synonymous with Puritanism, it was destined to be. Significant groups of Americans, however, usually as a consequence of some degree of persecution resulting from this Puritan chauvinism, resented the Puritanization of the United States. In the process of defining their own relationships to the development of the nation, representative Catholic, midwestern Democrat, and southern thinkers developed similar, though in important respects distinctive, critiques of New England's antebellum Puritan ideology. The southern critique, to be considered in the next chapter, analyzed Puritanism as part of a comprehensive process of secularization. The Catholic and midwestern Democratic critique, to be examined presently, focused more narrowly on the Puritanization of American politics. Calling attention to the growing pluralism of the United States, they demanded that all groups participate in the definition of America's identity and the realization of America's destiny. Because Puritan persecution was the one experience all three groups shared, their principal contribution to interpreting the Puritan tradition in the nineteenth century was not constructive but destructive; destructive, that is, of the normative identification of Puritanism with Americanism. Today, they offer especially penetrating insight into the cultural significance of the antebellum Puritan ideology as well as the difficulties any absolutist mode of thought encounters in a democratic society.

From the mid-1830s through the Civil War, midwestern Democrats likely to have sympathy with the wartime Copperhead or Peace movement, and Catholics, were the most vocal opponents outside the South of New England's habit of equating its own religious and political convictions with the principles that should guide the preservation of the Republic. These critics were not necessarily less pious than those they accused of "political religionism," nor less convinced that the United States existed under a special dispensation from God. The Democratic party and its organ the *Democratic Review*, supported the union of Christianity and democracy during the 1830s and were outspoken proponents of the idea of America's providential destiny during the 1840s. The historian Rush Welter has recently demonstrated that Catholics readily accepted both doctrines as long as "American mission, immigrants' choices, and republican safety all came together in support of the idea of an American asylum."[1] But both groups objected to the attempt by any single segment of the populace to claim exclusive insight into the will of God and to dictate its position to the rest of the nation.

Catholics Condemn Puritan Fanaticism

In many ways Catholics stood in a peculiar position vis-à-vis Puritan New England. On the one hand, Catholics agreed with "the fundamental principle of the Puritans . . . that the Law of God is Supreme in the State." They could identify with the intention of "the Pilgrim Fathers [who] . . . incessantly aimed at the introduction of the religious element into Massachusetts politics" and with "our Revolutionary Fathers [who] did nearly the same thing." On the other hand, however, Catholics did not always find their own interpretation of divine law to be in accord with that of the Puritans or their descendants. The Puritans, "being most bigoted Protestants . . . did not fully understand what the law of God was," but that did not stop them from trying to impose it on others.[2] This was painfully evident during the antebellum period in the outbreak of evangelical sectarianism that developed into Know-Nothingism and in what Catholic spokesmen consistently referred to as the abolitionist "frenzy" that caused the Civil War.

The Protestant crusade against Catholicism sought to save both Christianity and republicanism from the authoritarianism of popery, allegedly the epitome of religious intolerance and tyranny. Yet from the Catholic point of view, Protestant sectarianism posed a much greater danger to American religious and political values than did popery. Bishop John England of Charleston, South Carolina, witness to the spread of Calvinist evangelicalism in the South as well as in the North in the early 1830s, feared the national consequences of the fanaticism of the elect, "the more sanctified and perfect of the land, as they esteem themselves; who leagued together in a holy covenant, to wage a war of extermination against infidels and Roman Catholics." His fears deepened as a result of the burning of the Charlestown, Massachusetts, convent in 1834 and the controversy about the sexual conduct of nuns and priests ignited by the Maria Monk publications of 1836 and 1837. Tracing both incidents to the

---

[1] Rush Welter, *The Mind of America, 1830–1860* (New York: Columbia Univ. Press, 1975), 63–64.

[2] "The Religious Element," *Boston Pilot*, December 10, 1853, p. 4.

"hypocrisy," "tyranny," and "bigotry" of Puritan intolerance, England spoke for many Catholics who began to question the nation's commitment to liberty of conscience. The "Puritans of our day" threatened political as well as religious freedom, according to England, by submitting to state legislatures proposals to exclude Catholics from holding public office. Such "puritanical legislation" was a betrayal of the liberal tenets of the democratic creed that American Catholics struggled to adapt to the requirements of their faith. Rather than embodying the spirit of liberalism, Puritanism seemed to Catholics to be the principal source of illiberalism in American life.[3]

As the Protestant crusade accelerated and became organized into the Know-Nothing movement, Catholics broadened their attack from exposing the discrepancy between republican principles and sectarian reality to condemning the entire history of Protestant dissent as subversive of religious and political order. Especially during the heyday of Know-Nothingism in the 1850s, local incidents often triggered an outpouring of ancestral anti-Protestant, usually anti-Puritan, sentiment. In 1849, New York public school teachers were fined for not reading the Bible in the classroom, proof that the "spirit of New England Puritanism is as active, and at times as ferocious, as it was two centuries ago."[4] In the same year, the Eliot school case in Boston reminded Catholics how weak was the principle of religious liberty among Reformed Protestants and how strong the spirit of religious persecution:

> In the same spirit that made Calvin burn Servetus in Geneva; that ravaged France and martyred Ireland—the same spirit that hanged Quakers in Boston, and whipped women through eleven towns of Massachusetts, stripped naked to the waist and tied to a cart's tail, a few weeks ago tortured a Boston Catholic boy during half an hour, in one of the public schools of this city, to compel him, contrary to the instructions of his father and the requirements of his religion, to join in repeating an interpolated Lord's Prayer, and a dislocated decalogue.[5]

Similarly, political preaching by such Protestant crusaders as Lyman Beecher evoked memories of the strain of fanaticism within Christianity that tried to promote justice by unjust and unholy means: "What *can* you say," the editor of the *Boston Pilot* asked, "to a crowd of men who tell you, as the Albigenses, the Wickliffites, the earlier Anabaptists, and

---

[3] "The Republic in Danger," *The Works of the Right Rev. John England, First Bishop of Charleston*, 5 vols. (Baltimore: John Murphy, 1849) IV: 16; "Bigoted Boston," *ibid.*, V: Appendix, 328; "The Republic in Danger," *ibid.*, 41.

[4] "New York Schools, Another Outburst of Puritanism," *Boston Pilot*, October 29, 1859, p. 4.

[5] "Lecture on Religious Liberty delivered in New Orleans by Dr. Nichols," *Boston Pilot*, May 21, 1859, p. 4.

many others did; that when they murder and revolt, they know that they are breaking the law, but that a higher law tells them not to obey any magistrate who is not a saint . . .?"[6]

The past, then, prepared American Catholics to find a much closer relationship than most New England reformers would have admitted between nativism and pietism on the one hand and abolitionism on the other. Catholics did not distinguish between the ostensibly conservative nativist and pietist crusades and the ostensibly liberal antislavery movement; nor did they believe it was mere coincidence that Know-Nothingism and abolitionism both became most aggressive during the 1850s. On the eve of the Civil War, from a city in whose memory the Know-Nothing riots of the mid-1850s were still strong, the Catholic *Louisville Guardian* summed up the struggles of the decade:

> No impartial observer of the times can fail to mark the pestilential intermeddling with other people's business, which has been so prominently displayed by the Yankee Puritans of the North, and which has contributed more perhaps than any other cause to bring about the present terrible crisis in our political affairs. . . . Instead of preaching the Gospel of peace and love, the Northern preachers have taken up the exciting political topics of the day and have fanned the political discussion, which is now threatening us with all the horrors of civil war.[7]

The relationship between Know-Nothingism and the slavery question was in fact more complex than Catholics fully realized. The imputed attitude of Catholic immigrants toward slavery affected, but in different ways, the thrust of the Know-Nothing movement, both North and South. In Massachusetts, for example, Protestants who were abolitionists persecuted Catholics because of their alleged sympathy for slavery, whereas Virginians suspected Catholic workers of opposition to all apparent oppression of the laboring class. In reality, Pope Gregory XVI's 1839 apostolic letter *In Supreme Apostolatus*, condemning the slave trade, said nothing about the Church's attitude toward domestic slavery in the United States or elsewhere. As a consequence, local bishops and the Catholic press had to interpret for themselves the proper application of the principle of the letter to the American situation, with varying results. Until the Civil War broke out in some cases, until the Emancipation Proclamation in others, the Catholic church generally agreed, however, that slavery was an undesirable institution but that its abolition would best be left to the working of Providence. This satisfied neither northern or southern nativists.[8]

[6] *Boston Pilot*, November 2, 1860, p. 6.

[7] Quoted in *Boston Pilot*, February 16, 1861, p. 2.

[8] Cuthbert Edward Allen, "The Slavery Question in Catholic Newspapers, 1850–1865," United States Catholic *Historical Society Historical Records and Studies* 26 (1936):

Ultimately, Catholic attitudes toward slavery, abolitionism, and Puritanism were formed as much in Ireland, from where the majority of Catholics had come, as in Rome or the leading dioceses of the United States. Although Daniel O'Connell, the leader of the Irish independence movement and a hero to many Irish Americans, gave his support to the British antislavery movement, most Irish Americans were unenthusiastic about abolitionism. The relation of abolitionism to British humanitarian radicalism on the one hand, and to the Protestant reform movements in Puritan New England on the other, inclined Irish sympathizers to oppose uncategorically such "isms" and their adherents. As Joseph M. Hernon concluded in *Celts, Catholics, and Copperheads*, by the 1850s most Irish nationalists, who had considerable influence on the attitudes of Irish Americans, "ha[d] no use for American abolitionism. For them, now, the dour Yankee reformers were the re-emergence of that Puritan fanaticism that had historically warred upon the Irish people, and that remained alien to the more richly expressive spirit of the church." Furthermore, to the extent that the South based its opposition to the "puritanical North" on the issue of states' rights, Irish in both the United States and Great Britain saw an analogy between the forced American Union and the forced union of Ireland and England.[9]

Once the American Civil War began, Catholics left little doubt as to what they believed was its principal cause. After over a year of discussion in the Catholic press and throughout the land, the *Boston Pilot* concluded: "The best minds of the country have decided that the doctrine of State Sovereignty is not more pestiferous to the perpetuity of the Republic than Abolitionism. The former is the parent of Secession; the latter helped the growth of Secession by its loud fanaticism. . . . In point of ideas Abolitionism is much worse than Secession."[10] And there was also little doubt that Puritanism was the origin of abolitionism. In 1861, the Irish-born bishop of Charleston, South Carolina, Patrick Lynch, wrote to the archbishop of New York, John Hughes, that by "taking up anti-slavery, making it a religious dogma, and carrying it into politics, [the Yankees] have broken up the Union."[11] Northern as well as southern Catholic press opinion, represented by the *Freeman's Journal* of New York and the *Catholic Mirror* of Baltimore, concurred. According to the

---

99–169; William G. Bean, "An Aspect of Know-nothingism—The Immigrant and Slavery," *South Atlantic Quarterly* 23 (October 1924): 319–34; Rev. Benjamin Blied, *Catholics and the Civil War* (Milwaukee: Benjamin Blied, 1945), chap. 2; Madelaine Hooke Rice, *American Catholic Opinion in the Slavery Controversy* (New York: Columbia Univ. Press, 1944).

9 Joseph M. Hernon, *Celts, Catholics, and Copperheads* (Columbus, Ohio: Ohio State Univ. Press, 1968), 67 and chap. 5.

10 "Abolitionism Overt Treason," *Boston Pilot*, June 7, 1862, p. 4.

11 *Ibid.*

outspoken *Freeman's Journal,* "The canting Abolition Puritans brought
on this war, on the issue that the barbarous Negro *slaves* at the South . . .
had the mission to see it done."[12] Even though Archbishop Hughes of
New York had established the *Metropolitan Record* after his break with
the combative tone of the *Freeman's Journal,* its editor, John Mullaly,
consistently presented Puritan culture as the source of both the anti-
Catholic extremism of Know-Nothingism and the abolitionism that precipitated the war.[13]

In November 1862, the *Boston Pilot* published a summary indictment
of the Puritan tradition entitled "Abolitionism a Philosophic Madness,"
occasioned by the announcement that the Emancipation Proclamation
would go into effect on January 1, 1863. The indictment concluded that
the fanaticism of the people of New England would not die out until the
"race" of New England's Protestants itself perished and, as later articles
suggested, was replaced by the race of Irish Catholics. Whether quixotic or
prophetic, the conclusion was based on both a historical and philosophic
analysis of Puritan New England culture, not unlike that developed by
southern commentators over the span of several decades.

"In the Eastern States of America," the article began, "the irrepres-
sibility of fanaticism is the most prominent mark that section of the
Republic is distinguished by. The first New England Puritans were
fanatics in religion on the other side of the ocean. . . . It was fanaticism
that gave the 'mayflower,' and other ships their living freights." Since
then, Puritanism had taken on a variety of new forms:

> It produced the 'blue laws'—the most absurd collection of statutes
> ever made;—it became ferociously inimicable to the Catholic
> faith . . . it rose up against the Irish in the borrowed vestments of
> Know-Nothingism, an unnatural politico-religious crime . . . aimed
> at forcing temperance as to liquor, on the whole land—a philan-
> thropy that has produced nothing but ridicule; and at the present
> time negro-worship is its attitude.

Its influence had also been extensive outside the arena of politico-
religious movements: "It has produced many a theological reprobate,—
has occasioned a number of suicides,—hundreds of different creeds have
sprung from it,—against political and religious freedom it has done the
worst injuries,—the education of the country it has done much to poison,
and the public interests it has again and again deranged." Whence came
this fanaticism of which there has been none "like it in the pages of
history"?

---

[12] From the *Freeman's Journal,* May 7, 1864, quoted in Allen, "The Slavery Question in
Catholic Newspapers," 160.

[13] Lauren Brown, *"The Metropolitan Record:* Its Life in Print, 1859–1873" (unpublished
M.A. thesis, University of Washington, 1973), chaps. 3 and 4.

It originated with the Puritans,—the early Calvinists of England. The miscalled Reformation brought it into *life*. It appeared at first a moral philosophic absolutism, that would dictate to church and state to the entire exclusion of every other sentiment; and that it still continues to be. . . . Their successors in North America have driven from existence all amenities, and they have often succeeded in making Church and State the unhesitating agents of its tenets.[14]

Irish Catholics were not the only members of the faith in the United States who hoped that this spirit might eventually be suppressed by the rise of competing cultural traditions. In one of its articles on the theme, "New England Left Out," the *Boston Pilot* printed a letter from Hartford, Wisconsin, in which the author identified with New England the "spirit of meddling with the local institutions of the different sections." The author then offered this compelling reflection on the likely outcome of such meddling: "And I, for one, differ from those who endorse that oft-repeated prediction that 'slavery would be the rock on which we would be severed.' I say that Plymouth Rock is the rock upon which we will be severed, if ever that ruinous event take place." Voicing the sentiment of both Catholic and midwestern anti-Puritans, the author concluded, "Too long have we followed in blind imitation the heresies of New England, the revolutionary section."[15]

Copperheads Condemn Puritan "Higher Lawism"

"New England Left Out" voiced the suspicion of Puritanism shared by German Catholics in the cities of Wisconsin and the surrounding area and the Irish Catholics of Boston and New York. Together, these groups provided support for the Copperhead movement that opposed the continuation of New England's crusade against southern slavery. In the present context, the Copperheads were less important as war resisters than as advocates of the cultural, political, and economic interests of those who sought to break the national hegemony of New England. Their attention to Puritanism bordered on the merely rhetorical, but their attacks added to the snowballing of opinion against identifying the basic principles of the American way of life with Puritanism.

Midwesterners constituted the majority among the Peace Democrats. Just as Catholics pointed to the historical persecution of the Church by Puritans in old and New England, midwesterners had experienced at least a generation of eastern disdain for the reputedly inferior moral code and religious institutions of the frontier. Among a vocal segment of the population of the Midwest, the Civil War finally provided the opportunity to challenge the notion that New England civilization was fundamentally

---

[14] "Abolitionism a Philosophic Madness," *Boston Pilot*, November 1, 1862, p. 4.
[15] "New England Left Out," *Boston Pilot*, March 21, 1863, p. 2.

superior to that of other parts of the nation. That is not to say that mid-westerners exploited resentment toward New England to curtail their support for the war effort of the North. In fact, one of the reasons for the demand during the second year of the conflict that the war be brought to a speedy end was the belief that New England did not field proportionately as many soldiers as the Midwest. Nor did even half of the region support the Copperhead cause. But the Copperhead movement did reflect the growth of a midwestern sectionalism that frequently defined itself in opposition to Puritan New England, and thus contributed to the pluralist challenge to the identification of Americanism with Puritanism.[16]

To a considerable extent the Peace Democrats of the Midwest simply used anti-Puritanism as a propaganda weapon to arouse support for their cause. The Copperhead press in Indiana, Illinois, Ohio, and Michigan exploited Catholic fears of the resurgence of Know-Nothingism by warning that, if the war were fought not only to restore the Union but to destroy slavery as well, the gratification of the religious fanaticism of abolitionism might lead to efforts by New England to make its sectional church a national one.[17] Nor were Peace Democrats above making rhetorical use of Catholic hatred of the name of Cromwell, going as far as to compare Abraham Lincoln with Oliver Cromwell's misguided son Richard.[18] When the Indiana Democratic convention met in 1862, following a grand jury investigation of the activities of the underground Copperhead organization the Knights of the Golden Circle, the Indianapolis *State Sentinel*, *Illinois State Register*, and Springfield *Illinois State Journal* reported the party's apprehension that the Republicans were conducting secret society scares in the spirit of the old New England witchcraft hunts.[19] Copperhead Congressman S. S. Cox of Ohio remarked a year later that "the miserable fanatics of 1691–2 . . . have their imitators in the zealots of today—those minions of power who spy about to accuse and arrest those who differ with them in politics."[20] If not particularly fruitful insights into the nature and role of Puritanism in American culture, such instances of anti-Puritanism attested to a visceral

[16] Wood Gray, *The Hidden Civil War: The Story of the Copperheads* (New York: Viking Press, 1942), chap. 3; Frank Klement, *The Copperheads in the Middle West* (Chicago: Univ. of Chicago Press, 1960); Earle D. Ross, "Northern Sectionalism in the Civil War," *Iowa Journal of History and Politics* 30 (October 1932): 455–512.

[17] Klement, *The Copperheads in the Middle West*, 32, and a letter to the *Columbus Crisis* by former Illinois governor John Reynolds, cited in Gray, *Hidden Civil War*, 115.

[18] Edward G. Ryan in the Milwaukee *Daily News*, July 2, 1863, quoted in Klement, *Copperheads in the Middle West*, 99, and a Chicago *Western Railroad Gazette*, June 13, 1863, account of attempts by Illinois governor Yates to silence the Copperhead sentiment in the state legislature, cited in Klement, *ibid.*, 66.

[19] Klement, *Copperheads in the Middle West*, 149.

[20] Samuel Sullivan Cox, "Puritanism in Politics" (Washington, D.C.: Library of Congress, 1863), 3.

suspicion of New England's most revered heritage, a suspicion that continued to color the political rhetoric of antieastern movements such as Grangerism in the postwar years.

The conjunction of the issuing of the Emancipation Proclamation and the arrest of the Ohio Copperhead leader Clement Vallandigham in 1863 brought on the height of the Peace Democrat movement. In response to the freeing of slaves in territories occupied by Union troops, the Democratic party of Douglas County, Illinois, wishfully prophesized that the Emancipation Proclamation would be "the entering wedge which will ultimately divide the middle and northwestern states from our mischief-making, puritanical fanatical New England brethren, and finally culminating in the formation of a Democratic republic out of the middle, northwestern, and southern states."[21] And in answer to the imprisonment of Vallandigham, his Ohio Democratic colleague, Samuel Sullivan Cox, delivered to the Democratic Union Association of New York his "Puritanism in Politics," which could very well have served as a position paper for commentators who had observed for years what they believed was the insidious influence of Puritan New England civilization on the life of the nation.

It was most appropriate that Cox clothe his defense of Vallandigham in terms of a criticism of the Puritanism of his persecutors, for Vallandigham had himself once remarked that he was "inexorably hostile to Puritan domination in religion or morals or literature or politics."[22] The opening paragraphs of "Puritanism in Politics" left no doubt that Cox intended an equally comprehensive attack from the point of view of the "men of the West," who objected to the political domination of the "Constitution-breaking, law-defying, negro-loving, Phariseeism of New England." The tendency to make "saints by statutes, and Paradises out of politics" and "to make government a moral reform association" threatened "to undermine the structure of our civil society." Equally reprehensible, when "Puritanism introduced the moral elements involved in slavery into politics [it] thereby threw the church into the arena." "Our Christianity," Cox continued, "therefore, became a wrangler about human institutions. Churches were divided and pulpits desecrated." By disregarding the fact that slavery was "a part of the Providential order," the "new evangel" of abolitionism also threatened to undermine the basis of republican religion.[23]

---

[21] Quoted from the Springfield *Illinois State Journal*, March 10, 1863, in Gray, *Hidden Civil War*, 125.

[22] Cited from the *Cong. Globe*, 37 Congress, 2nd Session, Appen., 58, along with other instances of his anti-Puritanism in Klement, *Copperheads in the Middle West*, 6–7. Vallandigham's brother also mentions this hatred of Puritanism in Rev. James L. Vallandigham, *A Life of Clement L. Vallandigham* (Baltimore: Turnbull Bros., 1872), 59, 80–81, 97.

[23] Cox, "Puritanism in Politics," 4, 11, 7, 5–6.

Cox made skillful use of arguments exposing the secularization of the Puritan impulse offered by the Calvinist Congregational minister Nathan Lord, who had to resign his New England pulpit when he supported slavery as a divinely ordained institution. Lord believed that the decline of Puritanism from piety to moralism had, paradoxically, narrowed rather than widened the separation of church and state in America. This opinion confirmed Cox's own conclusion that "the idea of Puritan politics is that sins should be reformed by the State, and that the State should unite its functions practically with the church for the propagation of moral and religious dogma." As a result of the practice of Puritan politics, not only had both politics and religion become corrupted, but, in the words of Lord, the glory of all that America stood for "has departed":

> Our Christianity has become secular, and our secular glory has been dimmed in having lost the reflection of a more spiritual light. We have substituted speculation for faith, and our speculative discussions have been degraded into angry wranglings. We have made God and man to exchange places: His institutions and His constitutions we have interpreted by the 'higher law' of our conceits. We have converted the Sovereign Law Giver into a politician. We have discussed by our own standards and determined by vote how it is best for Him to carry on His government of the world. We have inquired not what He has willed and done, but what it is expedient for Him to will, and say, and do, according to a master, a party, or a school. We have popularized our creeds, measured principles by their utilities, and God himself by His supposed subserviency to our ideas.

Once reduced to this man-centered morality, Puritanism had nothing to offer but a code embodying the ethical imperative of seventeenth-century Puritanism in its form but containing no universal or transcendent sanctions applicable to all in its content.[24]

Only the war, Cox complained, had fully convinced Americans outside New England that "a system of public morality prevalent in one section, is not the guide of duty under the Constitution." But an astute student of past and present history—such as Cox no doubt thought himself to be—would have realized that Puritanism had never contributed anything worthwhile to the spread of republican politics or republican religion in the United States. It had, instead, attempted to draw all authority unto itself. In colonial times,

> the wrong-headed fanaticism which refused to consider the Democratic Gospel of Love, clung to the old Testament with its *lex-talionis* for its codes. Familists and Baptists, Quakers and deluded people who gathered sticks for fire on a Sunday, were all punished by the harsh Jewish code. All other crimes not punished by the law already enacted were to be attended to according to the old Bible, as the

[24] *Ibid.*, 5, 8.

fanatic interpreted it, the 'higher law' of their own judgment being the interpreter. This is the boasted Pilgrim Democracy!

More recently, the history of Puritanism

has run the round from orthodoxy, beginning with Mucklewrath Cheever, brimful of vengeance against sins, 'he had a mind to,' and winds up in the infidelity and scepticism which Parker preached and Emerson sung. Exalting this life above the next, it is not content with the order of Providence. It must assume control of the Chariot of the Sun, and direct all its shine and shadow.

Whatever authority Puritanism had claimed as arbiter of public morality could not and should not survive this descent into denial of providential law.[25]

Cox's look at the recent religious history of New England was insightful, but his memory of the hope his own party had had in the ability of Puritanism to provide a foundation for both a Christian and a democratic Republic was short. Democrats, too, had once believed that Puritanism would remain theologically orthodox enough to instill republican virtue and, at the same time, become politically liberal enough to realize the full meaning of popular sovereignty. When, by the Civil War, it had apparently done neither, the Peace Democrats concluded that, at best, Puritanism was an object lesson in the impossibility of making politics in a plural society serve a single standard of morality without precipitating conflict.

During the war, Peace Democrats reached the same conclusion other Americans would reach after the war: the separation of church and state would have to mean the divorce of religion and politics. Catholics did not as readily agree, but then neither had this formal issue been their foremost concern. Catholics had hoped for a more liberal spirit in the public life of the United States, toleration in religion and equal access to economic and political power. But they encountered a much less secular and much less liberal environment than they expected, for which they held Puritanism accountable. Puritanism was a residue of the sixteenth- and seventeenth-century struggles American Catholics no longer expected to have to fight. But fight they must, as long as Protestants believed that the United States rather than the Catholic church was the symbol of God's Kingdom here on earth. Thus to Catholics, Puritanism was an object lesson in the dangers of what today is recognized as elite revolutionary ideology.[26]

The Catholic and Copperhead indictments of the American Puritan

[25] *Ibid.*, 10, 12.
[26] Michael Walzer treats the English Puritans somewhat in this way in *The Revolution of the Saints* (Cambridge, Mass.: Harvard Univ. Press, 1965), as does Eric Voegelin, although much less favorably than Walzer, in *New Science of Politics* (Chicago: Univ. of Chicago Press, 1952).

tradition were important in discrediting antebellum Puritan ideology, although the precise weight and nature of their influence is difficult to measure. Even at their most rhetorical, Catholic and Copperhead criticisms of Puritanism reveal a familiarity with Puritan history and the dimensions of what we have called Puritan ideology that strikes the modern observer as impressive and gives credence to charges against New England's Puritan imperialism. Whatever the particular fate of antebellum Puritan ideology, the more general influence of the Puritan tradition would certainly be difficult to erase from America's civic culture. At their most analytical, Catholic and Copperhead criticisms of Puritanism exposed the deep running contradiction between the formal separation of church and state in America and the nation's pride in being a God-fearing people. Whereas *Harper's* magazine feared the threat to the purity of religion implicit in this contradiction, Catholics and Copperheads feared the threat to political power only recently unshackled from ecclesiastical domination. From this vantage point, they saw more clearly than northern Protestant commentators that the United States's commitment to religious toleration might have to mean toleration of separate realms for religion and politics—the cultural rather than the racial practice of separate but equal—not competition among religiously-identified groups for political leadership. When, and if, that separation occurred, the Puritan tradition could become a captive of either realm; another, as yet unformed, realm; or possibly no realm at all.

5

The Secularization of Orthodoxy

Moderate northern Protestant reformers, Catholics, and midwestern Democrats were full participants in America's demonstration that fidelity and republicanism were not only historically compatible with, but also necessary to, each other. They also agreed that antebellum Puritan ideology in its maturest expression went too far in the direction either of Christianity or liberal democracy, hence threatening by its extremism to belie this essential historical truth. Southerners who commented on Puritan ideology, while also trumpeting the charge of extremism, rejected the historical presupposition giving the charge force. By mid-century a highly articulate body of southern opinion insisted that liberal democracy was compatible only with false, rather than with true, Christianity. Furthermore, Puritanism in this southern view was not extreme religionism imposed on politics, as it was to Catholics and Copperheads; nor was it the politicization of religion, as it was to *Harper's*. Puritanism was, instead, the corruption of both religion and politics, brought about by a secular force common to both. As irreligion and as radicalism, antebellum Puritanism revealed to southern thinkers that the real historical dynamic of northern development was not the struggle to accommodate religion and politics in pursuit of a Christian Republic, but the triumph of the profane over the sacred, of Antichrist over Christ.

As part of the larger process of articulating its own positive cultural identity between 1830 and 1865, southern thinkers developed the idiosyncratic but powerful analysis of antebellum Puritanism just summarized. The analysis always remained secondary to the more constructive task of creating a basis for southern cultural distinctiveness in a way Copperhead, and even Catholic, analysis never could be. As a consequence of its being an instrument of the South's own ideology, then, the secularization theory must be approached with caution. But it is worth recalling that the South's contempt for Puritanism was bred by familiarity, especially familiarity with the imminent dangers of self-righteousness. Rather than as a projection of its own self-righteousness onto northern reformers, however, the South's indictment of Puritan secularism can be seen as a shrewd conservative's recognition that religious orthodoxy and moral purity have traditionally required the support of political authority, and never more so than when they begin to erode. Where orthodoxy and purity have a higher priority than toleration, in the civil as well as the spiritual realm, then political authority becomes the servant of the dominant creed rather than the moderator among many. And where more than one creed vies for control over the political authority, conflict is inevitable.

Southern Christians and New England Infidels

Five months after the outbreak of the American Civil War *DeBow's Review*, published in New Orleans, carried as its lead article "The Puritan and the Cavalier; or, the Elements of American Colonial Society." The author admitted that the North and the South had once "fought side by side on behalf of liberty"; but he insisted that "viewing the parties to this compact now . . . we can clearly perceive that there existed, in the very beginning of our national career, principles inherited from our colonial settlements which were so discordant as to render it impossible for any power, less than a military despotism, to perpetuate the Union."[1] The discordant principles represented by the Puritan and the Cavalier were not, according to *DeBow's*, simply projections of other familiar sectional tensions but were independently rooted in the divergent religious histories of the North and the South. Southern thinkers concluded from these histories that theologically and ecclesiastically Puritanism contained the seed of degeneration from religion to ideology, whereas southern religion embodied a respect for order and authority that deepened its commitment to orthodoxy.

In his influential *Lecture on the North and the South*, delivered before the Young Men's Mercantile Library Association of Cincinnati in 1849, Ellwood Fisher stated the case for the contrast between Puritan and Cavalier in its simplest form: "under the operation of their respective institutions the religion of Massachusetts has receded from one of the most strict to one of the most relaxed systems of the Protestant faith—while Virginia has advanced from one of the most indulgent, to one of the stricter forms of religious discipline."[2] In the following decade other southerners came to

---

[1] "The Puritan and the Cavalier; or, the Elements of American Colonial Society," *De Bow's Review* 31 (September 1861): 210. This article was probably written by an English correspondent named Samuel Phillips Day for the London *Morning Herald*. It and "The Belligerents," *DBR* 31 (July 1861): 69–77, were later reprinted as part of Day's diary *Down South: or an Englishman's Experience at the Seat of the American Civil War* (London: Hurst & Blackett, 1862). See Rollin G. Osterweis, *Romanticism and Nationalism in the Old South* (New Haven, Conn.: Yale Univ. Press, 1949), 148 on the authorship of "The Belligerents." In his diary Day, of course, dropped the use of the first person plural, which hid the fact that he was not an American from readers of *DeBow's Review*.

[2] Ellwood Fisher, *Lecture on the North and the South* (Wilmington, N.C.: Fulton & Price, 1849), 25. The *Southern Quarterly Review* noted the lecture in 1849 in "Review of 'Lecture on the North and the South'," 15 (July 1849): 273–311; also see reviews in *DBR* 7

believe that their "respective institutions" did not alone explain the receptivity of the North to Unitarianism, Transcendentalism, and other unorthodox ideas at the time that evangelicalism was triumphing in the South. Beneath the different religious institutions of South and North was a philosophical division between conservatism and liberalism: between respect for the order established by the accumulated experience of generations and the belief that "the individual man was . . . of higher worth than any system of polity"; between the sober conviction that man's nature is flawed and the faith that "would hurry man by unnatural stimulants towards unattainable perfection."[3] Perhaps George Fitzhugh described this difference most graphically in 1860 in *DeBow's Review* when he refuted the popular notion that the South and the North were divided by a "sectional issue." The dispute, he proclaimed, was "between conservatives and revolutionists; between Christians and infidels; . . . between the chaste and the libidinous; between marriage and free love; between those who believe in the past, in history, in human experience, in the Bible, in human nature; and those who . . . foolishly, rashly, and profanely attempt to 'expel human nature,' to bring about a millennium, to inaugurate a future wholly unlike anything that has preceded it."[4]

Fitzhugh was quite aware of the irony implied in his portrayal of the dispute between South and North. Like Ellwood Fisher, he was convinced, however, that in the two centuries since the settling of America the Puritan and the Cavalier had done something of a moral *volte-face*: "The Puritans of New England were at first more moral, religious, wise, prudent, and intolerant than we, but now negroes go to school with and marry white girls, Bloomers walk the streets, strong-minded women lecture against marriage and the Bible, and weak-minded men against everything orderly and respectable."[5] Fitzhugh and others believed that through the operation of some sinister dialectic, Puritanism had been turned on its head. Something within Puritanism seemed to generate its opposite: from an overstrictness in morals, Puritanism bred licentiousness; from deprivation and self-denial, resulted an excessive pursuit of wealth; and from religious fanaticism sprang infidelity. The impulse for this dialectic, southern thinkers generally agreed, was the Puritan insistence on the right of private judgment. As a consequence, their interpretation of the Puritan tradition focused on dissecting both the history and

---

(August 1849): 134–35 and *ibid*. 7 (October 1849): 304–16. As sectional conflict intensified during the 1850s *DBR* again turned to Fisher's lecture in "Ellwood Fisher on the North and the South," 23 (August 1857): 194–201.

[3] "Life and Character of Governor Endicott of Massachuesetts," *SLM* 14 (August 1848): 461; and "Political Religionism," *ibid*. 4 (September 1838): 558.

[4] George Fitzhugh, "Disunion within the Union," *DBR* 28 (January 1860): 4.

[5] George Fitzhugh, "The Old Dominion—The Valley of the Rappahannock," *DBR* 26 (April 1859): 372.

the logic of the Puritan expression of private judgment in relation to politics as well as religion.

The southern analysis of the idea of private judgment began with the recognition that, historically, the Puritans had defended conscience in the "knowledge to discern their rights" against what they believed was the corrupt and false authority of the established Church of England.[6] Having perhaps in mind the current specter of New England Transcendentalism, southern commentary proceeded to point out that the Puritan assault on the established order did not end there: "the radical revolutionary ideas of Puritanism . . . were to secure universal freedom from all kinds of restraint, religious, social and political; everything to be subjected to the test of the reason of the individual."[7] History more than logic had driven the Puritans to proclaim the "universal freedom of opinion," at least in part because the revolution in religion precipitated by the Reformation had preceded the modern revolution in governments that established republicanism. Had the reverse been true, a Virginian writing for the *Southern Literary Messenger* suggested, "the disturbed elements of society might have once more blended peacefully together beneath the auspices of a common religion."[8] As it was, the right of conscience became simply one of many rights that modern political movements asserted against all established opinion and authority.

Despite the pressure of events beyond Puritan control, history, or at least the prevailing southern interpretation of history, could still judge Puritanism harshly, for the Puritans had not defended the right of private judgment responsibly. The Puritan proclamation of the right of conscience had not been disinterested. From the very beginning, the Puritan right of private judgment implied the private Puritan judgment of right against the allegedly wrong judgments of the established order. In 1837, a contributor to the *Southern Literary Messenger* observed that "from justly insisting upon thinking and acting for themselves, . . . [the Puritans] came . . . unconsciously and unconscionably, to claim the right of thinking and acting for others."[9] By 1860, a writer for the traditionally more militant *DeBow's Review* displayed a less tolerant, but more incisive, understanding of the psychology of the Puritan conscience: "each man having discovered that he alone was the true expositor of Scripture, felt it a sacred duty to compel every other man to think and to act on all subjects as he himself thought and acted." Puritanism replaced belief in the infallibility of "presbyters and synods . . . kings

---

[6] "The New England Character," *SLM* 3 (July 1837): 416.

[7] "Editor's Table," *SLM* 36 (February 1864): 124.

[8] "The Influence of Morals on the Happiness of Man, and the Stability of Social Institutions," *SLM* 4 (March 1838): 146.

[9] "The New England Character," 416.

and bishops" with belief in "individual infallibility."[10]

Just as individual infallibility became the expression of the Puritan idea of private judgment in religion, so military despotism rather than republicanism was the logical consequence of the idea of private judgment in politics. The psychology of the Puritan conscience also "requires of every man, if he believes he understands the art of government better than other people, to force other people to conform to his notions." Military despotism, the kind of force the Puritan applied in political matters, "grew out of Calvinism"—Calvinism, that is, of the old Puritan vintage rather than the new southern vintage.[11]

In its preference for a congregational polity Puritan Calvinism again displayed its despotic tendencies by extending the logic of the infallibility of the individual to include the infallibility of the congregation of true believers. The result was a general disrespect for all rules other than those that "each body of believers . . . may deem fit and proper."[12] In the American Republic the Constitution embodied a rule to preserve the religious freedom of all believers. Yet congregationalism neither inculcated obedience to rules regarding religion not established by individual churches nor provided mechanisms for disciplining clergy who violated the provision of the Constitution respecting religious freedom. As northern ministers increasingly preached abolitionism from the pulpit, congregationalism seemed to some southern thinkers to be a party not only to military despotism but also to religious tyranny:

> The great religious struggles of modern history have all been in the contentions between the principles of Calvinistic *insubordinantism* and Episcopal *subordinantism*. The first is iconoclastic in all things. The second teaches respect and reverence in all things. The first aids all efforts to destroy the Constitution. The second assists all efforts to maintain the Constitution. The advocates of the principle of episcopacy in church government, understand that it is only in and through the Constitution that their religious rights are permanently assured, and consequently, if they suffer the instrument to be invaded either in respect to negro-slavery, or in any other respect, the way becomes open to an invasion of those clauses that guarantee religious liberty.[13]

---

[10] "Bonaparte, Cromwell, and Washington," *DBR* 28 (February 1860): 142.

[11] *Ibid.*

[12] "The Study of History," *SQR* 10 (July 1846): 141.

[13] "The Relative Political Status of the North and the South," *DBR* 22 (February 1857): 128. Southern commentators had long been disturbed by the adoption of the antislavery position among influential northern ministers. See especially "Review of 'The Duty of Free States'," *SQR* 2 (July 1842): 130–77; "Domestic Slavery, Considered as a Scriptural Institution," *SLM* 11 (September 1845): 513–28; review of *A Key to Uncle Tom's Cabin*, in *SQR* 24 (July 1853): 214–54; "The War Against the South," *DBR* 21 (September 1856): 271; "Report on the Southern Convention at Savannah," *ibid.* 21 (November 1856): 550–53; and R. M. Johnson, "Religious Intoleration," *ibid.* 22 (February 1857), 166–80.

The principle of episcopacy, then, embodied historically in the Anglican and Catholic churches, enabled the Cavalier to be the true and faithful
supporter of religious toleration. In reality, however, the descendant of the
Cavalier, his moral and theological senses sharpened by the infusion of
Calvinism into southern religious life, inclined chiefly to defend only the
freedom to be orthodox, nay literal, in his interpretation of Scripture. The
biblical justification of slavery was a prominent feature of the avowedly
orthodox position from which many southerners attacked not only abolitionism but northern heresy in general.[14] Looking back upon the religious
developments of the antebellum period, the Southern Agrarian Frank
L. Owsley isolated in a few sentences of "The Irrepressible Conflict" this
particular aspect of the divided religious heritage of the nation, as understood by southern commentators both then and later. The portion of
Owsley's contribution to *I'll Take My Stand* cited here is particularly interesting as an expression of the lingering belief that the Puritan and the Cavalier had reversed their roles in the dramatic struggle between theological
latitudinarianism and theological orthodoxy:

> A scriptural and historical justification of slavery was called in to
> meet the general wrongfulness of slavery in the abstract. Partly as a
> result of this searching of the Scriptures there took place a religious
> revival in the South, which had tended heretofore to incline to Jeffer-
> sonian liberalism of the deistic type. The South became devoutly
> orthodox and literal in its theology. But the abolitionists were not
> willing to accept Biblical justification of slavery. There was an
> attempt to prove the wrongfulness of slavery by the same sacred
> books, but, finding this impossible, many abolitionists repudiated the
> Scriptures as of divine origin. Partly as a result, the North lost confi-
> dence in orthodoxy and tended to become deistic as the South had
> been. One could almost hear Puritan New England creaking upon its
> theological hinges as it swung away from its old position.[15]

Owsley was not suggesting that in swinging toward deism the North had
adopted Jeffersonian liberalism as well. He rather had in mind the transition to Unitarianism in many of those same New England pulpits from
which the hard truths of Calvinism once echoed, though it is questionable
whether those truths had ceased echoing for a majority of abolitionists.

The biblical justification of slavery was not the only sign of antebellum southern religious orthodoxy; nor could Puritan New England be
heard creaking on its theological hinges only because it began to question the divine origin of Scripture. With considerable reason, southerners
believed themselves more orthodox than northerners in the matter of

---

[14] See especially "Domestic Slavery" and the review of *A Key to Uncle Tom's Cabin* in
SQR 24 (July 1853).
[15] Frank L. Owsley, "The Irrepressible Conflict," in *I'll Take My Stand* (New York:
Harper & Row, 1930), 81.

who shapes history, man or God. The belief in Providence, once so very typical of the Puritan outlook in New England, seemed beleaguered by the man-centered ideas of romantic intellectuals. Southern commentators attributed romantic "man-worship" to the secularization of the idea of the right of private judgment, and their critique of "man-worship" became the most telling aspect not only of their analysis of the doctrine of private conscience but also of the development of the Puritan-Cavalier typology before the Civil War.

Many thoughtful southerners genuinely believed that in time Providence would oversee the emancipation of southern slaves: "If such by the Almighty fiat—if only from the chaos which must ensue from such a wreck, God will deign to execute his designs for this world—we are indeed pygmies in his hands, and must bow to the overwhelming destiny."[16] What they found reprehensible was the premature hastening of that day by those who "have assumed that . . . [they] are able to fathom the purposes of the Omnipotent . . . [who] with . . . [their] puny vision . . . would take in the infinite scheme of things, and dictate to the Almighty where, how, and when He shall do His own work."[17] It hardly surprised such southerners that northerners would presume themselves "wiser than God, and would reverse the ways of Providence,"[18] for in the words of a satiric poem entitled "The Northman's Cause" the idea prevailed in the North that

> Man, man alone, is God,
> And God impersonation but of Fate,
> Or but the type of human aggregate,
> Or name of master Impulse of the time:
> A needless sanction; but of force of use,
> 'Tis fitter to assert Supreme control
> For what is seen to be the course of men,
> In what was once the dreadful name of God.[19]

The references to fate and the deification of man in these lines suggest almost inescapably an allusion to the romantic apotheosis, in the Transcendental school of New England philosophy, of the Puritan idea that "everything . . . be subjected to the test of the reason of the individual."[20] As early as 1842, a contributor to the *Southern Quarterly Review* had defined the Transcendentalists as people who "decide the

---

16 "Negro and White Slavery—wherein do they differ?" *SQR* 20 (July 1851): 131–32.
17 "The Present Aspect of Abolitionism," *SLM* 13 (July 1847): 433. See also "The Designs of Black Republicanism," *DBR* 28 (March 1860): 268.
18 George Fitzhugh's review of *The Pioneers, Preachers and People of the Mississippi Valley,* in *DBR* 30 (March 1861): 270.
19 "The Northman's Cause," *SLM* 31 (December 1860): 414.
20 "Editor's Table" (February 1864): 124.

claims of religion, by reference to their own convictions of truth."[21] As more and more persons associated with the Transcendentalist school, such as William Ellery Channing, Theodore Parker, and finally, Ralph Waldo Emerson himself, joined the antislavery crusade, southern commentators came to identify the Transcendental "reaching into the realm of a *'higher excellence'* " with the abolitionist appeal to "higher lawism."[22] As clearly as any feature of cultural life in the North during the antebellum period, the appearance of Transcendentalism bore witness to the philosophical division between northern rationalism, based on an unyielding faith in the right of private judgment, and the southern reliance on experience and history and revelation as the true sources of wisdom.

What was the South, believing more in the wisdom of God's Providence than in the fanciful schemes of human reason, to do, when confronted with the practical application of rationalism to the question of slavery? "Is the South to sit content with this dispensation, not of Providence, but of Puritanism?"[23] In 1850, from the unlikely forum of the Southern Commercial Convention in Nashville, the Cavalier resorted to the formula of the Puritan jeremiad to try to chasten the North. A proclamation by that convention anticipated "the terrible denunciations of an outraged deity, and the fiery warnings which the benevolence of God still vouchsafes to the offenders," if northerners persisted in substituting "man for God, in the objects of their solicitude."[24] Thus, the Cavalier became the instrument for invoking the wrath of God against "those prophets of Baal who pretend to interpret in . . . [God's] name."[25]

Norman Cavaliers and Saxon Puritans

The irony of the South's viewing itself as God's instrument for chastening the North matches that of asserting the moral superiority of the modern Cavalier over the modern Puritan. Yet it, too, added a special dimension to the interpretation of the Puritan tradition in terms of the contrast between the Puritan and the Cavalier. As an American Civil War began to appear imminent, southern thinkers shifted their development of the Puritan-Cavalier typology from religious and philosophical differences to the historic struggle of the English Civil War in which the reformed Cavalier triumphed over the Puritan in the bloodless Revolution of 1688. This new emphasis not only encouraged southern anticipation of an early

---

[21] "Transcendentalism," *SQR* 2 (October 1842):453.
[22] "The Difference of Race between the Northern and Southern People," *SLM* 30 (June 1860): 404–05.
[23] John H. Means, "On the Destinies of the South," *SQR* 23 (January 1853): 195.
[24] "The Southern Convention," *SQR* 18 (September 1850): 232.
[25] "Review of 'The North and the South'," *SQR* 27(January 1855): 4.

victory over the North but also challenged the northern philosophy of history which placed the Puritans in the vanguard of Protestantism and Protestantism at the head of the coming millennium.

Early in 1860, A. Clarkson of Alabama referred to the Puritans and Cavaliers "in the revolution which temporarily changed the face of Great Britain something more than two hundred years ago" as the "ancestors" and "prototypes" of the parties then in conflict in the United States. The Puritan of old was "unfit for rational freedom," demonstrated by the "extremity of his principles going to the subversion of all society," his intolerance, and "the short duration of his power when attained." The "even wider extremes" of the modern Puritans' "social, moral, and political heresies" tended "to a yet more complete subversion of society and overthrow of the moral government of God." The Cavaliers, on the other hand, while originally displaying "many human failings," had, according to Clarkson, prepared their descendants for "perfecting the great work they began in 1688, establishing a free, representative, and constitutional republic, with an open Bible, and with the noblest, most cultivated and enlightened, and most Christian social system that ever existed."[26]

In the succeeding months, southerners increasingly drew analogies—some apt, many not so apt—between the political history of their own period and that of seventeenth-century England. "Charles I lost his head for crimes that were virtues by the side of those committed against Kansas," and "the perfidy of James II of England, and the ruling of his atrocious judges, seem honor itself when contrasted with the perfidy of the last James of our American presidents . . . [i.e., Buchanan]."[27] The Democratic party after 1856 had united "puritanism" and "agrarianism" by the "prayer of Cromwell," which always seeks to make others bow to Puritan purposes.[28] The excesses to which this union led reminded one *Southern Literary Messenger* contributor of the Puritan excess of another day: "The period in history . . . to which their present moral and political status bears the strictest resemblance, is that to which the North stands allied by ties of blood and race. The Roundhead scenes of the Cromwellian period[.]"[29]

During the 1860s, belief in "ties of blood and race" between Puritan and Saxon, Cavalier and Norman, replaced historical analogy as the interpretive basis for invoking the example and precedent of the English Civil War period. In the process, aspects of the analysis of a conflict of principles explicitly identified with the Puritan and Cavalier traditions

---

[26] A. Clarkson, "The Basis of Northern Hostility to the South," *DBR* 28 (January 1860): 8–11.

[27] "Why We Resist, and What We Resist," *DBR* 30 (February 1861): 27.

[28] "The Designs of Black Republicanism," 270.

[29] "Northern Mind and Character," *SLM* 31 (November 1860): 345.

were temporarily lost, though the substance of the division remained. Indeed, the notion of "ties of blood and race" facilitated adoption of a comprehensive philosophy of history dating from before the English Civil War, comparable to the prevailing romantic philosophy of history in the North that viewed the Puritan colonization of America and the American Revolution as the fulfillment of the Protestant Reformation. The Puritans, according to the southern interpretation, descended from the Saxons, whom the Cavaliers, descended from the Normans, had tried to convert to Christian orthodoxy since medieval times. One author, for example, recalled for the southern heirs to the Norman-Cavalier legacy that their "old Saxon enemy," before the victory of William the Conqueror at Hastings in 1066, "was heretical in the eyes of Rome" and that "the essence of that idea finally found its maturity in the rigid principles of the Puritans."[30]

In this context, the Norman-Cavalier became for a few southerners the defender of Counter-Reformation Catholicism in the South, rather than of a Calvinism untainted by Puritan fanaticism. "Puritan iconoclasm finds its most stalwart foe in Catholic conservatism," one author wrote, having perhaps been influenced by George Fitzhugh's earlier prophecy that a "conservative reaction in politics, in law, in morals, and in religion" was about to accomplish the "rolling back of the reformation! Of reformation run mad."[31] But, for other southerners, the Norman-Cavalier could just as readily become the ancestor of the French Huguenot from whom many southerners, including the DeBows, were descended. And this interpretation of the Norman legacy served to clarify why Calvinism per se was compatible with conservatism, but Puritanism bred radicalism.

Southern commentators found it particularly important to distinguish southern French Calvinism from northern Puritan Calvinism as they tried to explain the peculiar nature of New England Puritanism. In 1853, for example, a contributor to the *Southern Quarterly Review* was most careful not to hold the French Huguenots in South Carolina responsible for the "Americanization" of the city of Charleston through the spread of the "Puritanical spirit." He granted that the Huguenots, like the Puritans, had "simple and 'unworldly' habits," but they did not carry those habits to such an extreme as to look "upon anything bearing the name of *pleasure* suspiciously and askance." Neither did the Huguenots forever repeat the old Puritan refrain that "life is but a pilgrimage." Catholics and Huguenots, according to the author, differed fundamentally in religious matters from the Puritans, who believed that "religion is not a principle which we are to take with us into Life and the World to

---

[30] "The Conflict of the Northern and Southern Races," *DBR* 31 (October–November 1861): 393.
[31] "The Designs of Black Republicanism," 270; Fitzhugh, "Disunion within the Union," 5.

guide, purify and strengthen us in intercourse with our fellows, but a sentiment which we must shut ourselves up from the world in order to indulge in it [sic] without distraction." In other words, Puritanism did not treat religion as an "informing spirit," as did Catholicism and French Calvinism, but rather as "an almost selfish gratification."[32]

In 1861, George Fitzhugh evidently recognized that the explanation of the Civil War as a conflict of philosophical principles primarily religious in origin required the assimilation of the southern Huguenot tradition into that civilization broadly described as Norman-Cavalier. He suggested that perhaps it had been the Huguenot influence—rather than, for example, the more likely Scotch-Irish—which, by the middle of the nineteenth century, had elevated the southern Cavalier to a higher moral plateau than the New England Puritan. French Calvinism had certainly proven itself more loyal to true religion than Puritan Calvinism: "With clear judgments and strong convictions . . . [the Huguenots] have known no disposition to interfere improperly in the judgments and convictions of other people. How favorably they contrast with the Puritans of the North, who began by persecuting people who would not conform to their faith, and are ending by having no faith at all—whose religious convictions were too strong in the beginning; and whose infidel convictions are now as obtrusive and intolerant as their former religious bigotry."[33] Most importantly, in addition to elevating the Cavalier, the political moderation and religious orthodoxy of the Huguenot also affirmed that Calvinism per se did not necessarily incline a people toward the democratic excesses and religious infidelity associated with Puritanism in New England.

The most serious wartime exponent of the "ties of blood and race" explanation for the Puritan-Cavalier conflict, J. Quitman Moore, believed that the political conflict beneath the religious and racial differences between Norman and Saxon explained why conservatism was compatible with Calvinism but not with Puritanism. His synthesis of the Saxon-Puritan's more complex motives deserves quotation in full:

> When the ecclesiastical power of England was withdrawn from the Vatican and transferred to Canterbury, this Saxon element became the fortress and arsenal of that violent and fanatical party of political and religious revolutionaries known as Puritans, Independents, or Presbyterians. . . . The Puritan became to protestantism what the Jesuit was to catholicism—the slave of one despotic idea, and the secret foe of all government, society and institutions that stood between him and the consummation of his gigantic conception. To this party eagerly attached themselves all that restless, selfish, arrogant and ambitious class, which commerce had elevated to sudden

---

[32] Review of *Anglo-American Literature and Manners*, in *SQR* 23 (April 1853): 406–9.
[33] George Fitzhugh, "The Huguenots of the South," *DBR* 30 (May–June 1861): 517.

importance, with no principle but their own passions, no opinions but their interests, and no faith but their fanaticism. And the machinations of this presbyterian or Puritan party, was but a herculean effort of the Saxon to wrest from the Norman the scepter of empire, making religious fanaticism only the cloak for concealing his political designs.[34]

Bringing his account of this conflict up to date, Moore continued to emphasize its fundamentally political implications. From the racial hostility between Norman and Saxon emerged a party conflict between Cavalier and Puritan or Roundhead that was not, however, resolved by the English Civil War. The Puritan was, and continued to be, "at once a religious fanatic and a political agitator and reformer . . . [who] could conceive of no government but the rule of the Saints; and form no other idea of the principle of civil liberty than what the leveling philosophy of the covenant taught." The Cavalier, on the other hand, was, and continued to be, "the builder, the social architect, the institutionalist, the conservator—the advocate of rational liberty and the supporter of authority against the licentiousness and morbid impulse of unregulated passion and unenlightened sentiment."[35] Even the later introduction of Calvinism into the Cavalier's religion could not pervert his conservative political instinct.

Two wartime writers for the *Southern Literary Messenger* also revealed the shift from the racial and religious to the political explanation of the Norman-Saxon, Cavalier-Puritan hostility. One author identified the real contestants as "Progressive Democracy" and "a sort of Patrician Republic."[36] Frank A. Alfriend, on the other hand, admitted that the battle of "ethnological principles" represented by the Puritan and the Cavalier was of considerable importance in interpreting the history of the United States since 1776. But ultimately, he, too, believed that that battle was just a phase of "the great question arising from the principles upon which rest the social organization of the two sections." Because "excessive popular power" derived from Puritanism, Alfriend was agreeable to using the term Puritan to describe the principle of democratic social organization in the North. But as a corollary he insisted that the term Cavalier be linked with the idea of a patrician society in the South, rather than, say, with a morally superior and religiously more orthodox culture, as it had been before the war.[37]

George Fitzhugh was one southerner, however, who never lost sight

---

[34] J. Quitman Moore, "Southern Civilization: or, the Norman in America," *DBR* 33 (January–February 1862): 5.

[35] *Ibid.*, 7–8.

[36] "The True Question: A Contest for the Supremacy of Race, as between the Saxon Puritan of the North, and the Norman of the South," *SLM* 33 (July 1861): 21, 24.

[37] Frank A. Alfriend, "A Southern Republic and a Northern Democracy," *SLM* 35 (May 1863): 287, 284.

of the original meaning of the Puritan-Cavalier typology that he himself did so much to popularize. Recognizing how widely the terms Puritan and Cavalier had become identified with parties during the American Civil War, he chose to apply fresh labels to the philosophical division between North and South once these party issues were "dead" in 1866. Yet, he still traced that division to the Puritan rejection of the authority of the Church of England, an authority that, based on tradition and experience, could have circumscribed the Puritan reliance on private judgment. Bereft of the salutary effect of such authority, "reason is everywhere indulged in bolder speculations." "Reason so far predominates, at the North, over faith, usage, custom, habit, prescription and authority," Fitzhugh concluded, "that we do no injustice in styling the people of the North 'Rationalists'—rationalists in religion, in politics, in agriculture, in law, in medicine; in fine, rationalists in all the pursuits and conduct of life." As a consequence, in the aftermath of the destruction of the Puritan and Cavalier parties, the most appropriate names for the principles represented by the North and the South were Rationalism and Conservatism.[38] In a sense, this had always been the true nature of the conflict—indeed the major distinction between the Puritan and the Cavalier—but now that the war had stripped away the institutional and customary differences between the sections, this underlying philosophical difference was once again clearly exposed.

The South's Critique Ignored

In their development of the Puritan-Cavalier typology, southern conservatives expressed a truth basic to all genuine conservatisms in the modern age, that religion is the foundation of a lasting social and political order.[39] Their rendering of the Cavaliers' religious history enabled them to validate the social and political order of the South; their rendering of the Puritans' religious history enabled them to condemn that of the North by exposing the secularization of the religious culture that both reflected and informed the rapid spread of egalitarianism and democracy. Many New Englanders shared the conservative insight of their southern critics, striving throughout the romantic period to link the rise of republican religion and institutions to the Puritan tradition. But, Puritanism could only withstand this identification by submitting to moralization and politicization. The South's articulation of the Puritan-Cavalier conflict could have provided a perspective from which to judge the capacity of the religious culture of New England to survive intact

---

[38] George Fitzhugh, "Virginia—Her Past, Present, and Future," *DBR* 1 (new series) (February 1866): 179–80.
[39] Russell Kirk, *The Conservative Mind* (Chicago: Henry Regency, Gateway Edition, 1960), 7.

these pressures of secularization, but because the typology was part of the South's creation of a separate identity, it was largely ignored.

The same year in which the editors of *Harper's* matured their thinking about the responsibilities of Puritan citizenship and the advisability of constituting a theocratic government in the United States, the journal also, however, offered one of the few serious northern responses to the South's portrayal of the ancestral antagonism between Puritan and Cavalier. "The New England Confederacy" set out to refute the claims of southerners who, "for more than thirty years . . . have endeavored, for unholy purposes, to excite sectional animosities by disparaging the Puritan character and exalting that of the Cavalier." To do so, it reprinted as definitive a comparison of the Puritan and Cavalier penned by George Bancroft in the first volume of his *History*:

> Historians have to eulogize the manners and virtues, the glory and the benefits, of chivalry. Puritanism accomplished for mankind far more. If it had the sectarian crime of intolerance, chivalry had the vices of dissoluteness. The knights were brave from gallantry of spirit; the Puritans, from the fear of God. The knights obeyed the law of honor; the Puritans harkened to the voice of duty. The knights were proud of loyalty; the Puritans of liberty. The knights did homage to monarchs, in whose smile they beheld honor, whose rebuke was disgrace; the Puritans in their disdain of ceremony, would not bow at the name of Jesus, nor bend the knee to the King of Kings. Chivalry delighted in outward show, favored pleasure, multiplied amusements, and degraded the human race by an exclusive respect for the privileged classes. Puritanism bridled the passions, commanded the virtues of self-denial, and rescued the name of man from dishonor. The former valued courtesy; the latter justice. The former adorned society by graceful refinements; the latter founded national grandeur on universal education. The institutions of chivalry were subverted by the gradually increasing weight and knowledge and opulence of the industrious classes; the Puritans, rallying upon these classes, planted in their hearts the underlying principle of democratic liberty.[40]

Harper's apparently did not question whether a portrayal of seventeenth-century Puritans, composed in the heyday of romanticism's reconstruction of the Puritan tradition, accurately characterized the nineteenth-century radicals bearing the same name almost thirty years later. The presumption of linkage was indicative of how confident the North was of its destiny in 1862. And in retrospect it was also prophetic

[40] "The New England Confederacy," *Harper's* 25 (October 1862): 633, 634–35. The quotation is from George Bancroft, *The History of the United States*, I: 322. Also see "American Principles," *Harper's* 14 (February 1857): 410; "The American Mind," *Harper's* 15 (October 1857): 692; James Russell Lowell, "Self-Possession vs. Prepossession," *Atlantic* 8 (December 1861): 761–69; Samuel Osgood, "Institutions and Men," *Harper's* 26 (January 1863): 273–77; "The President's Message," *NAR* 98 (January 1864): 260.

of how ill-prepared to defend the Puritan tradition the traditional leaders of American culture would be after the war, when destiny did not unfold exactly as Puritan ideology had envisioned it. Failing to take the substance of southern criticism—or of Catholic and Copperhead—seriously while Puritan ideology was in the ascent, northern intellectuals found it difficult not to resign themselves to it when they, too, realized the extent to which the Puritan tradition had been seriously compromised by concessions to secular pressures.

6
The Origins of the Genteel Tradition

In September 1867, W. F. Allen, editor of the *Nation*, warned the Republican party of the historical limitations of its Puritan ideology: "In the stormy times through which we have just passed, the uncompromising zeal of the Puritan element has been of the most signal service. Now the situation is changed. We have passed from the revolutionary stage to that of construction, and we need above all things, calmness, moderation, and a regard for the rights of all."[1] Later the same year, amidst a revival of the crusade against personal vice and sounding ever so much as if he had internalized the Catholic and Copperhead as well as the southern critiques of the Puritan tradition, Allen offered an explanation of why Puritanism suited social revolution but not social construction. Puritan ideology, Allen claimed, tried to change the social order in accordance with a limited vision of transcendent truth and in response to the personal experience of moral and spiritual anxiety. It aimed at uprooting evil more than planting the seeds of virtue and was motivated by guilt rather than by idealism. Puritanism was, in other words, the expression of an essentially religious mentality. But as religion declined in importance in New England as well as within the culture as a whole, a politics based on Puritanism, Allen concluded, threatened to succumb to manipulation by secular "ideologues or moralists."[2]

Those Americans who still valued the Puritan legacy in the period between the end of the American Civil War and the outbreak of World War I in Europe, at first tried to reverse the course run during the romantic period and to redefine Puritanism as a religious and philosophical tradition. They did so, however, under circumstances considerably less favorable than those surrounding the antebellum reinterpretation of Puritanism. Puritanism was still a reality before the Civil War in the sense that its theological, political, and cultural imagination was still a vital inheritance that the forces of liberalization and secularization had to combat. By the end of the Civil War, these forces had, for the most part,

---

[1] W. F. Allen, "The Dangers of the Republican Party," *Nation* 5 (September 19, 1867): 223.

[2] *Ibid.*, 232–33, and W. F. Allen, "Puritanism in Politics," *Nation* 5 (October 3, 1867): 275.

triumphed, and Puritan ideology had spent its vitality, W. F. Allen's fears notwithstanding. The spiritual and moral universe to which Puritanism, including the antebellum Puritan ideology, attested, and in which it flourished, seemed to have collapsed. The North had won the Civil War and freed the slaves but at a staggering cost in lives, destruction of land, civil disorder, speculation and corruption, and political violence. The victory had barely been celebrated before the South began to reshackle the freedmen in Black Codes and northern politicians acrimoniously debated the terms on which the two sections would be reunited. For most American thinkers the credibility of Puritanism remained lost, at least in the ideological form the romantics tried to give it.

But as a form of expression, however anachronistic, of seemingly intuitive truths about the world, Puritanism gradually regained, among well-educated easterners, some of its credibility and even some of the spiritual power it earlier submitted to secularization. Its spiritual appeal became decidedly more personal than collective, more psychologically reassuring than morally or politically inspiring, more directed against excessively naturalistic modes of thought than against immorality or injustice. And rather than acquiescing to secularization to narrow the gap between reality and the ideal as the antebellum Puritan ideologues had done, postbellum "Puritan" thinkers tried to resist secularization by professing that the ideal existed in reality wherever individuals acted in response to universal truths. The attitudes identified as Puritan by post-Civil War thinkers derived much more from a need to salvage traditional bearings than actively to defend and revitalize them, however. They were also much closer to the periphery than to the center of post-bellum cultural change. But the persistence of any positive associations with Puritanism after the war is noteworthy and the particular character of these associations indicates how deeply entrenched was the belief that Puritanism was the American expression of significant human values. This belief, especially in its turn-of-the-century form, was the heart of what George Santayana labeled the genteel tradition.[3]

Naturalism and the Renewal of Calvinism

The reappropriation of the Puritan tradition began in response to the rise of naturalistic explanations of the natural and social world. Naturalism, and especially evolutionary theory, at first seemed to support, rather than to deny, some of the most fundamental beliefs of Calvinist theology. To those seeking universal lessons from the observation of the past, the message of evolutionary theory was that evil was still powerful in the world,

---

[3] George Santayana, "The Genteel Tradition in American Philosophy," in *The Genteel Tradition*, ed. Douglas L. Wilson (Cambridge, Mass.: Harvard Univ. Press, 1967).

that morality higher than expedience was difficult to realize, and that becoming too attached to things of this world was unwise. By sharing Calvinism's conviction of moral order and fatalistic tone evolutionary theory strengthened Calvinism's claim to be an expression of universal truth. And reinforcing one another, evolutionism and Calvinism together offered a welcome corrective to the subjectivism of romantic religion and romantic optimism about man's ability to perfect himself and his society.

The first point of contact between evolutionary theory and the postbellum renewal of Calvinism was an appeal to reason and the rational discovery of an objective reality:

> The central or fundamental philosophical truth which underlies the mental and moral culture which the age requires is the truth of the moral order of the universe. Human life belongs to an actual order,—a cosmos, not a chaos; and this order is a moral order and tends to prefer truth, justice, and righteousness. The opposite error, which has misled a large portion of American society, is the opinion that the moral order to which man's life belongs is subjective only. . . . That is what is really fatal in unbelief in our time,—not the rejection of the creed of my church or yours, but the loss of the perception and assurance of the truth that the laws of nature and the inevitable working of the forces of the universe are hostile to falsehood and injustice; that extreme individualism is now abnormal and self-destructive; and that fraternal or social justice is provided for and required by the constitution of things, by the laws of an order which man did not make and cannot change.[4]

As Christians have explicated divine revelation in terms of the science and philosophy of the age, so now at least some American religionists set out to find in the objective world described by evolutionary theory evidences of the divine truth about the God-man relationship.

The idea of Providence was the principal means by which American Calvinists had expressed the objectivity of the Christian cosmos. Evolutionary law was, at the very least, analogous to providential law as an explanation for the motivating force of the world. Returning to an understanding of Providence common a half-century earlier, Samuel Osgood observed in 1878 that the mood created by evolutionary theory "shows . . . the drift of recent thought in the search for absolute reality, and its disposition to find in impersonal law and unconscious force the inexorable sovereignty which it has ceased to find in the Divine Personality and Providence."[5] For Christians who did not allow the naturalism of Darwinian evolution to replace the supernaturalism of revelation, evolutionary theory simply complemented the idea of Providence. The .

---

[4] "Certain Dangerous Tendencies in American Life," *Atlantic* 42 (October 1878): 385.

[5] Samuel Osgood, "Pessimism in the Nineteenth Century," *NAR* 127 (November–December 1878): 465.

Harvard philosopher Francis Bowen, for example, found no conflict between the Christian and evolutionary cosmologies, both of which described "the successive evolution from ancestral germs of higher and higher forms of life and mind." He was confident that the attempt to divest the evolutionary process of "God's providence and incessant creative action . . . by reducing it to a blind mechanistic process . . . resting solely upon the two unfounded assumptions of a battle for life and of the necessary survival of the higher organisms over the lower one in that contest . . . must be regarded as an ignominious failure."[6] Two decades later, in 1897, the editor of *Harper's* confirmed that failure: "This is still God's world. It is just as much His world as it was in the first century of our era. Providence still orders the affairs of man. The civilization that we have attained is the evolution of His purpose."[7]

Just as Calvinism and evolution both refuted the romantic view that the world was of man's making and had no objective reality other than that attributed to it by the individual, they also denied the proposition that evil was not an integral part of that reality. The philosopher and historian John Fiske noted that "the Calvinist is much more nearly in accord with our modern knowledge than are Plato and Mill," regarding the existence of radical evil in an evolving universe. He also implied that, conversely, the pessimistic and fatalistic conclusions of modern science should actually be welcome as supporting traditional Calvinist religious faith: "Suppose we could bring back to earth a Calvinist of the seventeenth century and question him. He might well say that the God which Mr. Mill offers us, shorn of the attribute of omnipotence, is no God at all. . . . Nay, more, the Calvinist would declare that if we really understand the universe . . . we should find scientific justification for the supreme and victorious faith which cries, 'Though he slay me, yet will I trust him.' "[8] And just as Samuel Osgood had approved the renewed appreciation of the working of impersonal laws in the natural world, so too he welcomed the sobering effect of the pessimism engendered by the theory of evolution because "it cautions men against over-sanguine anticipations, rash adventures, and romantic visions, and leads them to recognize the limitations of their own intelligence and power in the facts of Nature, and the vanities and vices of their fellow men."[9]

If evil were an integral part of reality, what then of the Calvinist, and especially the Puritan, drive to destroy evil? Some postbellum thinkers worried that modern science, lacking the "loop-hole" of the doctrine of

---

[6] Francis Bowen, "Malthusianism, Darwinism, and Pessimism," *NAR* 129 (November 1879): 463.

[7] "If Christ were to Come to New York," *Harper's* 96 (December 1897): 151.

[8] John Fiske, "The Mystery of Evil," *Atlantic* 82 (April 1899): 437–38.

[9] Osgood, "Pessimism in the Nineteenth Century," 472.

election, justified the existence of evil. In "The Great Delusion of Our Time" in the June 1904 *Atlantic*, John H. Denison summarized the fears of those who otherwise found in evolutionism the familiar Calvinistic view of the world: what was new in the evolutionary view was "not that the world is on a primitive tooth-and-nail basis, but that it stands acquitted, nay, justified, by a verdict apparently based upon the doctrine of Evolution, and that conscience is discredited." But once evolutionary theory helped to reinstate Calvinism as intellectually respectable, the efficacy of the Puritan conscience might also be made compatible with modern science, just as had the doctrines of Providence and the existence of radical evil.[10]

To secularists, evolutionary theory refuted the idea of things permanent; but to religionists, the same theory necessitated the careful differentiation between what was transient and what, like the existence of radical evil, persisted in substance though it might change form. In 1904, a subscriber to the *Atlantic* contributed a charming testimonial to his conclusion that the Puritan conscience, and especially the Puritan impatience with evil, was as permanent a feature of the universal order as evil itself. In "New Thoughts on the Puritan Conscience" he wrote: "Whenever during all these years my conscience has become insupportably disagreeable, it has always been a relief to me to throw the blame of it upon the Puritans, and hope that when we had gotten a little farther from them such things would become impossible. I tried to think of it all as a piece of atavism and that I should get over it." But after thirty years of trying to deny these pangs of conscience, "a suspicion, half joyous and half sad . . . has come over me that perhaps it was not the Puritan conscience at all." During that time, the author continued, "I have felt just the possibility of the Puritan, living in the enlightened state above, doing what I never used to think a Puritan could do, laughing in his sleeve at us, and wondering how long it would take us witty people to realize that it was not his conscience we had gotten hold of but our own." Representing not just this individual response to the Puritans' testimony to conscience, but the response of a generation to the rediscovery of other Puritan truths as well, the author concluded by asking, "Why not give them credit for their youth, and admit once and for all their depressing contemporaneousness?"[11]

Once Calvinism and the Puritan conscience could be accepted as compatible with the liberal, scientific mind of the late nineteenth century, the immediate post–Civil War suspicion of political religionism

[10] John H. Denison, "The Great Delusion of Our Time," *Atlantic* 93 (June 1904): 725–26. Also see George W. Julian, "Is the Reformer no Longer Needed?" *NAR* 127 (October 1878): 240; "The Religious Conflicts of the Age," *NAR* 133 (July 1881): 42; "What is Pessimism?" *Atlantic* 61 (May 1888): 716–17; "Ancient and Modern Fatalism," *Atlantic* 88 (September 1901): 432.

[11] "New Thoughts on the Puritan Conscience," *Atlantic* 94 (November 1904): 718–19.

began to dissolve. In the late 1860s, many Americans, northern as well as southern and midwestern, believed Puritan moral absolutism had been responsible for leading the nation into a war that obfuscated the problems of public ethics and loyalty, unleashed the materialistic instinct, and proved irrefutably that life was a struggle for survival. But the rejuvenation of Calvinism, to which naturalism paradoxically pointed, ultimately revitalized Puritan ethics as well. Although the Gilded Age did produce the extreme political religionism of New England in the American Protective Association nativists and such moralizing firebrands as Anthony Comstock, the Puritan conscience also and perhaps more representatively expressed itself in moderate appeals for a return to basic moral principles. The desire for moral education in the public schools, the reexamination of the theocratic ideal by political theorists, the incorporation of orthodox theology into the Social Gospel, and a crusade against materialism undoubtedly seemed immoderate to many postbellum Americans. But in contrast to the demands made by the Puritan conscience before the Civil War, the postbellum Puritan conscience rested more on the religious, rather than the political, foundation of the Puritan impulse, and self-consciously recoiled from fanaticism.

The Tamed Puritan Conscience and Genteel Idealism

The granting of the franchise to millions of formerly enslaved blacks and the naturalization of large numbers of immigrants pointed up to thoughtful Americans, as nothing had since the spread of Jacksonian democracy, the difference between the right of suffrage and the more comprehensive idea of citizenship. Four years after his retirement from the presidency of Yale in 1871, the political scientist Theodore Dwight Woolsey emphasized the need for citizens to be educated in right judgment, if universal suffrage were truly to be the highest expression of political freedom. In addition to growth in general intelligence, true citizenship also required "an increased moral and religious purity."[12] Toward these ends during the 1870s, the evangelical National Reform Association supported a constitutional amendment that would have "recognized the Bible in our public schools by 'divine right'."[13]

It was not uncommon for those who wanted a more ethical education of the American citizen to cite the example of the Puritans. Some, like Erasmus Darwin Keyes, comrade and defender of the controversial General Winfield Scott, wondered whether modern Puritanism had the same capacity as colonial Puritanism to impart responsibility and brotherhood to common school education, for after "many disputes and rapid

---

[12] Theodore Dwight Woolsey, "The Experiment of the Union, with its Preparations," *Harper's* 51 (October 1875): 683.
[13] Julian, "Is the Reformer no Longer Needed?" 258.

change . . . the theory of the Puritans . . . is less characterized by the religious element than by political equality, or freedom[.]" Yet Keyes looked back to the earliest Puritans for confirmation that education in freedom demanded education in morality, and that religion was the surest foundation for a moral education.[14] Others, like Theodore Woolsey and Eugene Lawrence had no such reservation as Keyes's about the Puritan contribution to education. Woolsey praised the Puritans "who planted first of all the church, and the school by its side," who within a few years founded a college as a pattern for all that should follow afterward as "the best possible pioneers of a coming host of freemen." In his centennial *Harper's* article on "Educational Progress" Lawrence advanced an ideal for the public school not far removed from what the Puritans envisioned for religious instruction in a Christian Commonwealth. The link between them was the notion of a community of individuals who should "know and fulfill all the duties of a good citizen . . . obey the laws without constraint, and practice humanity, honesty . . . be trained to virtue, and cultivate self-control."[15]

The questions raised during the public school debate converged with those examined by postbellum political theory, and especially by the "theocratic" view of the state anticipated by *Harper's* in the 1860s. The version of theocracy formulated in the post–Civil War period relied on an idealistic philosophy that explained positive law as a reflection of divine law. Elisha Mulford, for example, appreciated by his contemporaries but until recently neglected by historians, saw in the Puritan theocratic ideal the same kind of universal truth that the contributor of "New Thoughts on the Puritan Conscience" saw in the Puritan resistance to evil. Mulford was an Episcopalian and a Hegelian who, in *The Nation: The Foundations of Civil Order and Political Life in the United States*, sought to illuminate the implications of the Puritan notion of the state as Christian Commonwealth while dissociating it from the recent activity of political Puritans. He believed that "there is no other conception which has such power in the thoughts of men, and in this age it has the greater significance when it is drawn not from a school of puritan politics, but from those most widely separated from historical puritanism, and finds its expression in the literature of a people which is rising to great political might." Central to this conception was the idea of the state as a moral organism, nurturing in history the seed of its divine origin by subordinating the will of the individual not to the interest of the majority but to the positive good of the divine law that liberates man from external control: "The strength [of the Puritan] was in the confession of an invisible presence, a righteous and eternal will

14 Erasmus Darwin Keyes, *Fifty Years Observation of Men and Events, Civil and Military* (New York: Scribner's, 1884), 90–91.
15 Woolsey, "Experiment of the Union," 673; Eugene Lawrence, "Educational Progress," *Harper's* 52 (November 1875): 845, 851.

which would establish righteousness on the earth, and thence arose the conviction of a direct personal responsibility which could be tempted by no external splendor."[16]

Theocratic theory also converged with recurring interest in the relation of the pulpit to the political issues of the day in reflecting the belief that right citizenship and patriotism united religious and political duties. Although reminiscent of the debate in the late 1850s about the propriety of clerical advocacy of abolitionism, the interest had narrowed somewhat with the rise of the professional reformer and the political administrator who left the clergy little more to do than to exhort church members to the religious grounds of their citizenship. The theological basis for this exhortation in the late nineteenth century was primarily the Social Gospel. The Social Gospel was principally indebted to liberal Christianity, but it also found a tappable reservoir of moral enthusiasm in the Puritan tradition. Even before the publication in 1907 of Walter Rauschenbusch's influential *Christianity and the Social Crisis*, noteworthy among other statements of Social Gospel thought for its orthodox theology, some American religionists sought to incorporate the Calvinist themes of sin and judgment into their formulations of the Social Gospel. Two attempts in particular stand out as mediating between the revival of interest in theocratic government and the more subtle influence of the Puritan tradition on the Social Gospel: Elisha Mulford's *The Republic of God* and Robert Thompson's *De Civitate Dei*.

The *Atlantic* literary critic Peter Steenstra called Mulford's *The Republic of God* "beyond all question the most remarkable of recent publications."[17] In it, Mulford sought to complement the catholic political theory of *The Nation* with a catholic theology in which God was equally immanent and transcendent, and in which His immanent activity occurred in both the civil order and in private life. Most significant for the applicability of Puritan spirituality to this theology was Mulford's use of the "progress of the Pilgrim of Bunyan" as the archetypal expression of the truth that "there is something more and other than the mere struggle for existence," that history reveals the triumph of freedom in the life of the spirit. The record of the human pilgrimage also indicated the price at which human beings achieved this freedom: it revealed that "there is through the world the conviction of sin, of righteousness, and of judgment." When the Social Gospel needed to revive this lost spiritual sense of the weightiness of the burden to conform human life to the

---

[16] Elisha Mulford, *The Nation: The Foundations of Civil Order and Political Life in the United States* (New York: Hurd & Houghton, 1872), 23, 267–68; Mark E. Neely, Jr., "Romanticism, Nationalism, and the New Economics: Elisha Mulford and the Organic Theory of the State," *American Quarterly* 29 (Fall 1977): 404–21.

[17] Peter Steenstra review, *Atlantic* 48 (November 1881): 698.

ideal of the Kingdom of God on earth, it could and sometimes did turn to the Puritan tradition.[18]

In *De Civitate Dei: The Divine Order of Human Society*, the Presbyterian professor of theology at the University of Pennsylvania, Robert Thompson, offered one such synthesis of the Puritan idea of the divine origin of the state and the pilgrimage archetype with the spirit of the Social Gospel. Thompson had to tread a narrow course between the conservatism, verging on fundamentalism, of the Princeton Theology of the 1890s and the secular or, as Thompson called it, "lower" sociology, and he did it with erudition and sensitivity. Deriving the modern implications of the fact that "Calvinism in its heroic days was a social as well as a theological faith," and that "it was theocratic to the core," Thompson tried to make the "Covenanter principle of the headship of Christ over all things to his people" a "common and precious inheritance of all Calvinists, nay, of all Christians." In this, his thinking was more traditional than that of the other religionists. But calling *The Nation* "the greatest book of our political literature," Thompson also agreed with Mulford's more moderate premise that the key to understanding and directing history was the process of making human law approximate "the ideal of perfect righteousness."[19]

American Protestants more liberal in their thinking than either the Hegelian Mulford or the Presbyterian Thompson also believed that the Puritan tradition had important insights into the obligations of the state and the improvement of society in the late nineteenth century. Above all, the Puritan tradition brought what the Congregational minister and historian of Puritanism, George Fischer, called the "Puritan sense of the responsibility and seriousness of life" to reflect on all human problems.[20] The former obstacle to appreciating this Puritan truth, the undemocratic theology of the elect, had been discarded. The intellectual climate of the 1890s encouraged pursuit of all truths sustaining human beings in difficult times through the ages, and within the churches this phenomenon was further inspired by the spread of ecumenism accompanying the practical cooperation of the Social Gospel movement. One result was the revival among liberal Christians themselves of the Calvinist notion of a superintending deity. Writing in the *North American Review* about one of his generation's more prominent Social Gospelers, George T. Knight observed:

> Lyman Abbott has said that some of the most vigorous presentations of the severity of God's punishment are those which are spoken from

---

[18] Elisha Mulford, *The Republic of God, an Institute of Theology* (Boston: Houghton, Mifflin, 1881): 84–85, 135.

[19] Robert Ellis Thompson, *De Civitate Dei: The Divine Order of Human Society* (Philadelphia: John D. Wattles, 1891), 12, 14–15, 121.

[20] George Fischer, "The Elements of Puritanism," *NAR* 133 (October 1881): 335.

Universalist pulpits. It seems that the thoroughgoing liberals have matured their convictions, and have established due relations with the facts of moral government. . . . The thing to be desired as a remedy for the backboneless condition of some of modern theology, is not unlike the good old orthodox doctrine of fear and the sense of justice executed. . . . For a large number of the liberal orthodox, while they preach God's infinite tenderness in dealing with offenders, yet also as plainly and forcibly declare His equal and exact justice, the certainty of retribution in this world and the next.[21]

Another result, however, was the increasingly generous attribution of peculiar insight and power to Puritan principles having in them increasingly less of the traditional theological core of Puritanism.

In the December 1895 *Forum*, for example, the Congregational minister and president of Bowdoin College, William DeWitt Hyde, explained how the pilgrim principle offered a solution to the "lost unity of Christendom":

Whether through a Catholic church made democratic and representative, or through Protestant sects federated into an unsectarian and universal body; whether through an orthodoxy that is courageous enough to think its doctrines through to their rational foundations, or through a liberalism that is earnest enough to demand at all costs a genuine piety; whether through a socialized church or a spiritualized state,—the sublime sense of responsibility to the Absolute and Eternal source of truth and righteousness which the Pilgrim magnificently affirmed will never lack for men and institutions to claim it as their own.

This affirmation is not exclusively "The Pilgrim Principle and the Pilgrim Heritage"; yet, it was important to some Americans to be able to make such claims. Why?[22]

In 1897, the semicentennial celebration of Plymouth Church in Brooklyn and tribute to its minister, Henry Ward Beecher, crystallized both the problems inherent in the latitudinarian rendering of the Puritan theological tradition and the reason behind it. The historian Alan Simpson concludes his *Puritanism in Old and New England* with a quotation from Amory Bradford's Plymouth sermon, "Puritan Principles in the Modern World," to suggest that "with its conviction that righteousness ought to prevail, with its tendency to make the Puritan's own moral character a test of political fitness, with its pressure to turn politics . . . into a moral crusade" such an exercise "reminds us of the darkest blot on [the Puritan's] political record."[23] A late nineteenth-century reviewer of

---

21 George T. Knight, "The New Hell," *NAR* 179 (July 1904): 132–35.

22 William DeWitt Hyde, "The Pilgrim Principle and the Pilgrim Heritage," *Forum* 20 (December 1895): 488.

23 Amory Bradford, "Puritan Principles in the Modern World," *The New Puritanism* (New York: Fords, Howard & Hulbert, 1898): 85–86; Alan Simpson, *Puritanism in Old*

the Plymouth symposium registered the opposite complaint that Bradford's sermon was untrue to the Puritan tradition in its treatment of the worldly Beecher as "a Puritan of the Puritans."[24] Both Simpson and the reviewer misunderstood Bradford and "the new Puritanism." The essence of Puritanism, according to Bradford, had always been the "larger spirit which reveres God and seeks his will; which owns no authority but truth; which believes in righteousness and does right, and always and everywhere trusts the people"; and only it would provide guidance in solving the problems confronting American society at the turn of the century.[25]

To the keynote speaker of the ceremonies, Lyman Abbott, "The New Puritanism" applied what was best in the history of the Calvinist theology that Bradford believed embodied the continuity of the Puritan spirit. In addition to inheriting the liberal pulpit at Plymouth Church from Beecher, Abbott was a leading exponent of progressive Christianity who did much to contribute the evolutionary perspective to the reform impulse of the Social Gospel. Retrospectively, he could praise the theology of Jonathan Edwards and Samuel Hopkins because it stimulated religious revivals by developing in people "a profound sense, if a somewhat morbid sense, of their guilt and sinfulness" and "a very profound, if not altogether healthful, reverence for God." But his new Puritanism went beyond the old in expecting these expressions of the religious spirit from all rather than a few. It obliterated the distinction between the elect and the nonelect by preaching the universal ideal of human liberty, and it supplemented personal, spiritual religion with an emphasis on social morality. Finally, it made religion natural, not in the naturalistic sense but in the sense that it realized religion was part of man's created nature—just as Elisha Mulford and Robert Thompson viewed the state as a moral organism because erected by individuals whose political impulse was also part of their creaturehood.[26]

Both conservative and liberal Social Christianity saw in the Puritan tradition, however loosely rendered, the moral authority to impose a new discipline on society. Outside that tradition, no other nonsecular authority seemed to exist in the late nineteenth century. Nor was the centrality of discipline, and the indebtedness to Puritanism for it, confined to Social Christianity. What was essential in the new Puritanism of Social Christianity also inspired the individual self-discipline to which other Americans looked to combat late nineteenth-century materialism. Whether social or individual, the ethic of self-discipline required a spiritual

24 John W. Chadwick, review of *The New Puritanism*, in *Nation* 66 (February 17, 1898): 137.
25 Bradford, "Puritan Principles in the Modern World," 103.
26 Lyman Abbott, "The New Puritanism," *The New Puritanism*, 38–39, 50–51.

sensitivity missing from the imposition of moral authority before the Civil War, helping to explain post–Civil War America's generally more moderate response to the issues it sometimes shared with antebellum spokesmen for Puritanism.

Few critics of the United States in the 1870s doubted that the Civil War, with its suspension of specie payments and the speculation mania that followed, was the principal cause of the "intensely excited worldliness" of Americans in the Gilded Age. It was, indeed, an ironic outcome of the war intended as a moral crusade that would seal America's special relationship with the God of history. What made the prosperity of the period not a providential blessing but a moral blight was the spirit of "venality" with which some Americans pursued this newfound wealth and the extent to which others were made to suffer. And with the growth of corporate profits, politicians for the first time in the nation's development, according to Theodore Woolsey, could be bought in large numbers. Whereas once "our poverty was our integrity," now prosperity was the source of corruption.[27]

American critics of materialistic culture did not immediately look to the Puritan ethic of self-discipline as a source of the alternative values of the spirit, for another Puritan ethic had for so long legitimized material success. George Harvey, then editor of the *North American Review*, found the tradition of individualism, based on the Puritan "theory that striving for material success is wholly in unison with the worship of God," now poised between the "gross pursuit of wealth" on one hand and "the opposite and equally materialistic doctrine of socialism" on the other.[28] Loren Knox, author of the December 1909 *Atlantic* article "Our Lost Individuality," offered a different but related explanation of the American obsession with material success. The Puritan tradition of individualism was not as responsible for contemporary materialism, he believed, as an aimless rebellion against the Puritan ideals of duty and morality. Perhaps these ideals did foster "unnecessary self-immolation and suffering"; but to abandon them as an act of protest against Puritanism, as more and more Americans seemed to be doing, was to "lapse into moral anarchy."[29] Taking Knox's warning to heart, mindful of the affirmation of moral order accomplished by the postwar accommodation to evolutionary theory and inspired by the mature development of Social Christianity, some Americans eventually sought to revive the Puritan ideal of renunciation.

Could all citizens be expected to inherit the ideal of renunciation

---

[27] Woolsey, "The Experiment of the Union," 684.

[28] George Harvey, "Are We Unconsciously Becoming Socialistic?" *NAR* 188 (October 19, 1906): 822.

[29] Loren H. B. Knox, "Our Lost Individuality," *Atlantic* 104 (December 1909): 822–23.

and resist the temptation to satisfy their materialistic instincts, or would the example of a disciplined few be sufficient to strengthen the moral fiber of the United States as it entered the twentieth century? In a remarkable letter to the *North American Review* in 1898, Charles Ferguson argued for "A Democratic Aristocracy, or Voluntary Servitude" in which "a class of persons of superior capacity, who might enjoy the privileges and immunities of an upper class [would] willingly submit to the conditions of life that are imposed upon the lower class." Such an extraordinary step was called for, Ferguson believed, because "we have committed ourselves to two opposite and mutually destructive principles. . . . We go on asserting in an anachronistic way the ancient moral theory of the self-made man, whilst denying the necessary consequences of that theory—which is caste." To escape this contradiction the partial Christianity that taught that "the commonest and poorest life has an estimable worth" must be supplemented by "the deeper content of . . . the teaching that civil liberty is valuable only as preparing the way for higher and more interior liberty—the liberty of self-devotion" or voluntary service to others. This was one way of reconciling the Puritan ethic of individualism, on one hand, with the Puritan ethic of self-denial, on the other.[30]

The ethic of self-discipline and simplicity could, finally, serve the promotion of true democracy in America's relation with the rest of the world. It represented the only means, according to William Dean Howells, by which "the American of the newer order [after the Spanish-American War] [could] show how one may have all the advantages, and not lose touch with those who have had all the disadvantages." It might be unrealistic and even undesirable for such a prosperous nation completely to renounce its wealth, Howells reasoned, but it must try to live according to a modified ideal of self-denial. Americans had once stood alone among the peoples of the world for the principles of "universal liberty or instinctive justice," which kept them "faithfully to the tradition of poverty and its implication of self-denial." Now more than ever, as the nation's responsibilities in the world increased, it must not allow its economic good fortune arbitrarily to divide one people from another, either at home or abroad.[31]

The application of the Puritan ethic of moderation in the enjoyment of worldly prosperity to the nation's relations with the rest of the world consummated the tendency to both identify the Puritan tradition with

---

[30] Charles Ferguson, "A Democratic Aristocracy, or Voluntary Servitude," *NAR* 166 (May 1898): 636–38. For another kind of reconciliation see two *Atlantic* articles by Vida Scudder, "Democracy and Society," 90 (September 1902): 350–54 and "Democracy and the Church," 90 (October 1902): 525.

[31] William Dean Howells, "An Earlier American," *NAR* 172 (June 1901): 942–43.

the expression of the most universal truths and apply those truths in the most comprehensive and least sectarian way. Thus, a number of intelligent Americans were able to establish and maintain their moral bearings amidst postbellum pressures to, on one hand, resist all change and, on the other, assent to cultural and ethical relativism. Puritanism became part of the mentality preferring restraint and order to any of the late nineteenth-century ideologies, from Social Darwinsim to socialism. It could urge restraint and defend order because it had faith in the ultimate efficacy of ideals such as justice and brotherhood, as well as self-discipline. The Puritan tradition may not have become any better suited to social construction by the end of the century than it had been in the late 1860s; but by reaffirming its spiritual roots, it did offer to some Americans an alternative to the enthusiasms of "secular ideologues and moralists."

It was precisely the restraint and the uncritical idealism of this outlook, however, that later critics disparagingly referred to as genteel. Those who had little faith in human ability to order life, or those who turned their backs on the value of order altogether in favor of more experimental approaches to the problems associated with rapid modernization, found little to admire in the Puritan tradition after the war. In reality they constituted a majority of the nation's influential thinkers, though possibly not a majority of its citizens. To both the representatives and the critics of this genteel tradition, however, Puritanism represented one, if not the only, national heritage to which Americans could look for spiritual guidance as the United States entered the twentieth century.

7

Puritan History Demythologized

If any group in American society could be expected to have played a leading role in salvaging the Puritan tradition after the Civil War, it would be the historians. In the romantic period, George Bancroft represented well the interests of the dominant New England culture in establishing its most hallowed heritage as the foundation of American development. Not long after the Civil War, however, New England historians were among the first groups to experience the decline of their region. Simultaneously, they began to respond to pressures to professionalize the discipline of history, culminating in the training in and practice of the philosophy and methodology of so-called scientific history. The end result of imposing professedly objective standards of scholarship on the study of the Puritan past was, according to Theodore Clark Smith in a 1906 *Atlantic* article entitled "The Scientific Historian and Our Colonial Period," that

> when it becomes necessary to pass judgment upon the Puritans the influences of the present day are too strong to permit the retention of a vestige of the filial eulogy once customary. People simply do not like Puritanism and no longer respect it. It is more remote from the present, more difficult to appreciate than the spirit of the discoverers, the explorers, or the buccaneers. Probably no more difficult task is imposed upon the historical imagination than that of representing the Puritan mind in the seventeenth century without caricature or repugnance.[1]

The "people" who no longer liked and respected Puritanism were not, as we have seen, the genteel Protestant establishment for whom the Puritan tradition had become the purveyor of universal moral and spiritual truths; they were, in addition to Catholics, midwestern Democrats and southerners, secular-minded New England scholars. The view of Puritanism these scholars offered the public certainly reinforced the negative attitude accompanying the aftermath of the Civil War. But perhaps more importantly, it severed the emerging genteel mentality from Puritan history. Thus, as the nation entered the twentieth century, the Puritanism of the educated Protestant establishment would lack the link to what was then

[1] Theodore Clark Smith, "The Scientific Historian and Our Colonial Period," *Atlantic* 98 (November 1906): 709–10.

taken as historical reality, which might have given more credibility to its idealism.

Postbellum historians did not always condemn the Puritan past outright, but they did challenge what they referred to as the filio-pietist assumptions underlying what passed for historical scholarship in the romantic period. After the Civil War, Bancroft's *History* was still authoritative among New England traditionalists, and the transitional figure John Fiske tried to adapt evolutionary theory to the study of the origin of American institutions in the same spirit in which Bancroft used providential law. A more objective view of American Puritanism did not automatically triumph over the filio-pietist, but new historical methods so shifted the focus of Puritan studies that the presuppositions of filio-pietism gave way. By the late nineteenth century scientific history defined its subject matter so narrowly that New England's strongest continuing legacy, its culture, fell outside its purview and into that of literary criticism and its new sister field, literary history. In the following chapter we will see how these disciplines, while being somewhat more respectful of Puritanism's legacy than political history, also undermined the hope that a "New Puritanism" might revitalize the American spirit. Together, historical and literary scholarship showed Americans a side of the Puritan tradition that, although it might be accepted or occasionally even respected as having once been historically necessary, made the Puritan impulse seem very much the product of a bygone era.

The Problem of Theocracy and the Challenge to Bancroft

The legal writer and publicist John Codman Hurd, reviewing two lectures by the filio-pietist George E. Ellis for the *Nation*, announced in 1869 that the traditional explanation of the Puritan origins of American institutions was no longer acceptable to the post–Civil War generation. The Puritans' "honest and avowed purpose, from the beginning, [was] to identify church and state in the person of their chartered corporation," Hurd insisted. As a consequence, "nothing can be more senseless than the common recognition of Providence as exhibited in the designs of the Puritans. Providence showed itself against their purposes, even when it brought great things out of their purposes."[2] Yet, Americans celebrated the nation's first centennial during the 1870s without an adequate explanation of the transformation of Puritan purposes in the century-and-a-half before the Revolution. So, when John Fiske published his account of "New England in the Colonial Period" in *Harper's* in 1882, the historiographical transition from the filio-pietist to the scientific interpretation of Puritanism was just beginning.

---

[2] J. C. Hurd, review article, *Nation* 8 (April 1, 1869): 253.

Consistent with the new respect for scientific explanation, Fiske tried to offer a "rational" resolution of the accepted paradox that on one hand religious liberty was an unforeseen consequence of Puritanism and on the other "the democratic civilization of New England is the greatest legacy which Puritanism has left to the world." How, that is, could a consequence admittedly unintended be judged a great gift to the world? The filio-pietist answer, represented for example by George Bancroft and John Gorham Palfrey, was that Providence could use any means to achieve its ends, including theocracy to achieve toleration and democracy. In contrast, Fiske based his resolution on the reasonableness of the Puritan experiment in self-government, even though the form of the experiment had been theocratic. Theocratic self-government was a reasonable application of the law of self-government for the Puritans, Fiske believed, because its "ethical conception of society was simply that which has grown up in the natural course of historical evolution" and because the Puritans showed "shrewd political sense" in not tolerating "indiscriminately all sorts of theological opinions." The Puritans thus created a situation in which later generations could apply the principle of self-government ever more widely.[3]

Fiske echoed the scientific spirit of his age by conforming Puritan history to a rational law of evolution. But the publication of Brooks Adams's *The Emancipation of Massachusetts* in 1886 set historical thinking about American Puritanism on an even newer course by denying that the paradox Fiske tried to resolve existed at all. Adams turned on their heads the traditional filio-pietist rationalizations of how Puritan institutions had facilitated the spread of liberal principles, arguing that only in rebellion against Puritan institutions did liberalism triumph. In a letter to Henry Cabot Lodge, Adams wrote of *The Emancipation*: "It is not really a history of Mass[achusetts] but a metaphysical and philosophical inquiry as to the action of the human mind in the progress of civilization; illustrated by the history of a small community, isolated and allowed to work itself free."[4] Whereas Fiske's evolutionism allowed for the slow realization of the self-governing principle within international Protestantism, Adams's mechanistic determinism required that the logic of the Reformation work itself out with all due speed in the isolation of New England. And since the idea of the priesthood of all believers would not wait for the magistrates and clergy of New England to realize that "any concession to the right to reason upon matters of faith involved the recognition of the freedom of individual thought," a conspiracy of

[3] John Fiske, "New England in the Colonial Period," *Harper's* 56 (December 1882): 116–17, 111, 114, 119.

[4] Quoted in Thornton Anderson, *Brooks Adams: Constructive Conservative* (Ithaca, N.Y.: Cornell Univ. Press, 1951), 43.

the strong, the learned, and the politically powerful must have retarded
the actualization of Reformation logic, once the Bible was placed in the
hands of the people.[5]

Although Adams claimed that *The Emancipation* was a study of the
liberation of the New England mind from the control of a priestly caste,
it actually dwelt on the methods by which the clergy of Massachusetts
Bay tried to obstruct that liberation. Had Adams confined himself to his
original purpose, he would merely have interpreted as a positive development what the filio-pietist John Gorham Palfrey had, in spite of himself, already diagnosed in *History of New England* as the decline of
clerical authority and the declension of Puritan theology. But the sociology of power was Adams's true concern, demonstrated by his extended
proof that, when they were unable to make theocratic control heredi-
tary, the clergy had shifted its power from the politico-ecclesiastical
establishment to a monopoly of education. The clergy was unable to
maintain its control over thought during the eighteenth century, however, and out of the struggle between the common Puritans and their
priests arose the defense of the abstract rights of man embodied in the
Declaration of Independence. In concluding his account of the transition
from Puritanism to the Revolution, Adams then introduced a new Puritan paradox by admitting that clerical fear of the establishment of an
Anglican bishopric in New England in the 1760s allied "sacerdotalism"
with "liberality" to make Massachusetts a "hot-bed of rebellion."[6]

However commonplace it is to observe that students of the American
past received Adams's *Emancipation* as a breath of fresh air, the
Atlantic Monthly reviewer who wrote the following certainly made the
simile appropriate: "It is as if a fog of ancient continuance should sud-
denly rise from a landscape which had hitherto been seen only under a
veil; and show it as at once the same and not the same, the same and yet
surprising."[7] That the unveiling of priestly oppression was done by a
bona fide descendant of the Puritans seemed especially prophetic of
future Puritanism historiography, although a *Nation* critic speculated:
"Every censure which [Adams] utters will be quoted more for its parent-
age than its truth."[8] But New England needed a new look at itself and its
relationship to the development of the United States. Even the *North
American Review* was tiring of Palfrey's multivolume apologetic *History
of New England* as early as 1875, and by the time his fifth volume

[5] Brooks Adams, *The Emancipation of Massachusetts* (Boston: Houghton Mifflin,
1886), 2, chap. 1.

[6] *Ibid.*, 239, 259, 362.

[7] Review of Brooks Adams's *The Emancipation of Massachusetts*, in *Atlantic* 59 (February 1887): 252-53.

[8] Review of Brooks Adams's *The Emancipation of Massachusetts*, in *Nation* 44 (March
3, 1887): 190.

appeared in 1890, critical opinion generally favored Adams's social history to Palfrey's old-fashioned institutional history.[9] Mediating the shift
was the publication in 1889 of John Fiske's *The Beginnings of New
England*. According to a *Harper's* reviewer, *Beginnings* proved that
"admiration for the character of the Puritan people, who were so much
wiser and better than the Puritan rulers," made for better history than
Palfrey's but was also more moderate than Adams's because it took the
Puritans "on their own terms."[10]

Originally a series of lectures delivered at Washington University in St.
Louis, *The Beginnings of New England* traced the evolution of the ideal
of political representation from the Roman principle of incorporation,
through its Teutonic formulation, to seventeenth-century England, and
finally to New England. But it also indicated that Fiske had digested
Adams's *Emancipation*. Echoing Adams's explanation of the success of the
American Revolution in New England, Fiske attributed the preservation of
English freedom to the "unwonted alliance of intense religious enthusiasm
with the instinct of self-government and the spirit of personal independence." Rather than perpetuating this new paradox, however, Fiske
explained the "unwonted alliance" by the fact that all Puritans, common
people and rulers alike, regarded themselves as "chosen soldiers of Christ."
As a consequence, "as much as [the Puritan] loved self-government, he
would never have been so swift to detect and so stubborn to resist every
slightest encroachment on the part of the Crown had not the loss of self-
government involved the imminent danger that the ark of the Lord might
be abandoned to the worshippers of Dagon."[11]

Recent studies demonstrate that Fiske's interpretation of the Puritan
legacy to the Revolutionary period was more accurate than Adams's paradoxical one.[12] Adams's history, like the scientific histories soon to follow,
had difficulty attributing constructive influence to religion or taking religious influences on public life seriously, for that matter. This was also true
of Charles Francis Adams, Jr.'s *Three Episodes of Massachusetts History*
and *Massachusetts: Its Historians and Its History*. A booster of scientific
technology, Charles Francis Adams, Jr. made a second career of exposing

---

[9] Critical notice of John Gorham Palfrey's *History of New England*, in NAR 121 (July
1875): 280.

[10] Review of John Fiske's *The Beginnings of New England*, in *Harper's* 79 (October
1888): 802.

[11] John Fiske, *The Beginnings of New England* (Cambridge, Mass.: Harvard Univ.
Press, 1889): 61, 308, 310. Dagon was a Philistine and Phoenician god who was half man
and half fish.

[12] Alice M. Baldwin, *The New England Clergy and the American Revolution* (New
York: Frederick Ungar, 1928); Bercovitch, *American Jeremiad*, chaps. 4 and 5; Alan
Heimert, *Religion and the American Mind* (Cambridge, Mass.: Harvard Univ. Press,
1966), chaps. 8, 9, and 10; Strout, *New Heavens and the New Earth*, chap. 4.

Puritanism to the light of his own version of "scientific" history, in which "confusion disappears, all is logical, all is necessary, all is the subject and outcome of law."[13] In *Three Episodes*, Adams rejected Fiske's implied justification of religious persecution as a means of maintaining self-government. It "may be filial but it is not rational and it is not fair," Adams wrote, to insist that because a people believed itself chosen by God, it was able to advance liberation by imposing conformity.[14] In *Massachusetts: Its Historians and Its History*, Adams argued that the history of the Puritan colonies had contributed nothing to the unfolding of the law of freedom of conscience as the filio-pietists believed, although it had made a lasting contribution to the realization of the principle of equality before the law.

Adams knew that equality before the law was not the explicit goal pursued by the common Puritans who struggled against successive threats of clerical repression of freedom of conscience; but equality was, nevertheless, the final outcome of the upward development of the colony through the periods of the "theological glacier" and political organization of the state to the scientific or "fluorescent."[15] The failure of earlier historians to detect this progress in achieving equality before the law had resulted from the New England habit of imagining that earlier generations had more faithfully shared common ideals than the present generation. Ideals did not, Adams pointed out, have to be widely shared to succeed. The historians' fixation on the moral decline accompanying the excesses of freedom of conscience obscured, according to Adams, the positive contributions past conflicts made to equality and placed an unduly high premium on the peace and stability which the theocracy had allegedly achieved. Stability was, understandably, not one of the laws Adams saw fulfilled in his own time, and thus he questioned its efficacy in the past. Another limitation of the late nineteenth-century imagination surfaced when Adams had to conclude about the period of the "theological glacier" that "perhaps Hawthorne in his *True Tales*, his *Scarlet Letter*, and his *Twice-Told Tales* has best embalmed most of the facts with all of its romance."[16] Despite these problems and his decisive rejection of the Puritans' self-appraisal, Adams affirmed New England's contribution to one of the great themes of modern history by chronicling the struggle for equality before the law. And even though his contemporaries never unreservedly accepted his conclusions, he, along with his brother, Brooks, secured a place for a new, critical, even negative standard of judgment in the historiography of New England Puritanism.

---

[13] Charles Francis Adams, Jr., *Massachusetts: Its Historians and Its History* (Boston: Houghton Mifflin, 1893), 108.

[14] Charles Francis Adams, Jr., *Three Episodes of Massachusetts History* (Boston: Houghton Mifflin, 1892), 563.

[15] Adams, *Massachusetts: Its Historians and Its History*, 108.

[16] *Ibid.*, 94.

In retrospect, it is clear that the Adamses were no more free of bias toward Puritanism than the filio-pietists. They also were not really professional historians. But their role in the reinterpretation of Puritanism is worth underscoring. Filio-pietism assumed that Puritanism was a single seed containing all the possibilities for growth that American development later realized: American history was Puritan history writ large. This had been the view of Charles Francis Adams, Sr. His sons, Brooks and Charles Francis Adams, Jr., contrarily, believed that religious, social, and political phenomena obey their own laws and that the present stage of progress dictates which of these laws was destined to take priority over the others. Since the late nineteenth century was secular and democratic, the historian had only to indicate when and how Puritan theocracy capitulated to liberal democracy. In addition, the empirical method isolated the discrete forces at work in Puritan society and focused on the cleavages resulting from religious, social, and political differences among groups of Puritans. Thus, rather than the Puritan tradition unfolding, Puritan society fragmenting became the dominant motif of pre–World War I Puritanism historiography. Indicative of the emergence of this new perspective was the proliferation of popular articles and books about Puritan dissent and the witchcraft phenomenon.

Puritan Persecution of Dissent and the Decline of Filio-Pietism

Even though Charles Francis Adams, Jr. believed that the history of Puritanism in Massachusetts contributed nothing to the spread of freedom of conscience, his objection to the Puritan attitude toward dissent was the basis for his rejection of filio-pietism in other matters. The Puritan treatment of dissent, including witchcraft, stripped other students of Puritanism of their filial piety as well and simultaneously pointed up the deepest divisions within the colonial Puritan movement. Postbellum thinkers were both attracted to and repulsed by these aspects of colonial Puritanism. The desire for sectional reconciliation and the anticipation of celebrating the national centennial in 1876 were strong motives for finding the principle of toleration at work in the American past; yet, the new search for rational laws in history subordinated the needs of national identity to the test of objective truth, and antebellum critics of Puritanism had already begun to question the truth of toleration. In addition, the receptivity of Americans to spiritualist beliefs throughout much of the late nineteenth century inspired a popular interest in seventeenth-century witchcraft that the naturalistically informed mind of the professional historian was likely to greet as a challenge.[17] By the beginning of

---

[17] Paul A. Carter, *The Spiritual Crisis of the Gilded Age* (DeKalb, Ill.: Northern Illinois Univ. Press, 1971), and Sheryl Feldman, "The Shadows of Materialism: Occultism in the 1880s" (unpublished M.A. thesis, University of Washington, 1971).

the twentieth century, the questions of dissent and witchcraft no longer inflamed either the popular or the historical imagination, but as in the case of the nature of the Puritan legacy, decades of debate replaced a sympathetic with a more critical interpretation.

Filio-pietists did not treat dissent as a central issue in colonial Puritanism, but when forced to comment on it, they cautioned against applying nineteenth-century standards to the seventeenth century. In *The Genesis of the New England Churches*, the Congregationalist minister Leonard Bacon, for example, noted that in the very act of migration the Pilgrims had demonstrated the seriousness of their desire for toleration in an age of religious tyranny, and he portrayed the Pilgrim pastor John Robinson as the founder of the tradition of toleration in the New World.[18] Another Congregational minister, Henry Martyn Dexter, undertook the more difficult task of explaining the fate of dissent among the Nonseparatist Puritans of Massachusetts Bay. Responding to a request from the citizens of Sturbridge for the Massachusetts legislature to rescind the 1636 sentence of banishment against Roger Williams, Dexter took issue with the notion that Williams "was banished from the Massachusetts colony solely because he was the fearless and far-seeing advocate of religious tolerance, the apostle of 'soul liberty,' or, in the more modern phrase, of liberty of conscience."[19] Dexter agreed with John Gorham Palfrey that Williams's banishment was purely a question of what a sympathetic *Atlantic Monthly* reviewer described as "prudent consideration for the harmony and self-preservation of the colony."[20] Further simplifying the issue between Williams and Massachusetts, John Fiske suggested that the specific authority to give grants of Indian land, even more than clerical authority per se, was the divisive issue justifying Williams's banishment.[21] Whatever the particular case, defenders of both the Pilgrims and the Puritans concluded that the hardships suffered by those who were themselves dissenting emigrants gave the colonists the "unalienable right to do as they pleased" and were thankful that the colonists' pleasure was to try a "great political experiment" in self-government.[22]

Brooks Adams specifically criticized the histories by Dexter, Palfrey, and George Ellis for ignoring the popular outcry against the ecclesiastical "enslavement of the mind" in colonial Massachusetts. Protests against "the repression of free thought," disgust at tortures and hangings, and Quaker martyrdom resulted, according to Adams, in the ascent of the

---

[18] Eugene Lawrence, review of Leonard Bacon's *The Genesis of the New England Churches*, in *Harper's* 50 (December 1874): 129.

[19] Review of Henry Martyn Dexter's *As to Roger Williams and his Banishment from the Massachusetts Plantation*, in *NAR* 123 (October 1876): 474.

[20] Review of Dexter's *As to Roger Williams*, in *Atlantic* 38 (November 1876): 630.

[21] Fiske, "New England in the Colonial Period," 118.

[22] *NAR* review of Dexter's *As to Roger Williams*, 477.

popular cause of liberty of conscience by the late 1660s.[23] Whereas popular reaction to the persecution of Quakers was the pivotal event in the emancipation of Massachusetts for Brooks Adams, Charles Francis Adams, Jr. looked to the Antinomian controversy of 1637 as the formative clash between the "oligarchy of theocrats" and the people. Although "premature," this first "protest against formulas" gave Massachusetts an invaluable lesson in equality for all who had access to Scripture. Adams was not particularly partial toward Anne Hutchinson, whom he called the prototype of that "misty school" of women transcendentalists, for her claim to have personally received communication from the Holy Spirit. He much preferred the quieter rebellion of her brother-in-law, the Reverend John Wheelwright, whose role in the religious development of New England Adams likened to that of the nineteenth-century Unitarian William Ellery Channing. Nevertheless, by asking how "a woman's preference among preachers [the regenerate John Cotton] was . . . to be transmitted into a crime against the state," Adams set in relief what was to him the central problem of distinguishing between "personal liberty where the rights of others are involved, and license where those rights are not involved."[24] As the result of the banishment of Hutchinson and Wheelright, Adams concluded, the party of the deputies among the Puritans gradually asserted its prerogatives against the clique of clergy and magistrates who had tried to conflate the issues of liberty and license in the cases against the Antinomians.

In regard to the question of dissent in colonial New England, Edward Eggleston's *The Beginners of a Nation*, published in 1896, served much the same transitional role as had John Fiske's *The Beginnings of New England* in regard to the question of the Puritan legacy. In *Beginners*, Eggleston examined the life of Roger Williams as the key to both the limitations and the reaches of seventeenth-century New England Puritanism. Because he turned away from social history back to viewing the first fifty years of colonization as a period of state building, Eggleston had to admit that Roger Williams "was a thinker, a doctrinary, too far in advance of his age to be the successful organizer of a state." Expressing admiration for the "forehanded statesmanship of the Massachusetts leaders in strangling religious disturbances at birth," Eggleston also believed, however, that Williams was the prophet of the end of all religious disturbances. Familiar with contemporary historiography, Eggleston noted that each of the sixteen Puritan settlements in existence at the time of Williams's arrival in the colony was at a different stage of evolutionary development, meaning Williams's prophetic "championship of soul liberty as the weightiest matter of the law" affected each differently. Where the spiritual foundations of

[23] Brooks Adams, *Emancipation of Massachusetts*, 162–63, 177.
[24] Charles Francis Adams, Jr., *Three Episodes*, 367, 382, 385, 395, 493, 546.

the Puritan movement had already begun to crumble, Williams's union of
Puritan "moral aspiration" with a new spirit of "disengagedness" from the
particular form of the Puritan experiment pointed toward a new era of
individual freedom. In contrast to Brooks Adams, Eggleston paid little
attention to clerical efforts to forestall the spread of individual freedom;
but in contrast to Charles Francis Adams, Jr., Eggleston also realized that
the spirit of dissent from below was as much religious as political.[25]

Colonial Witchcraft as a Puritan Perversion

The phenomenon of witchcraft in Puritan New England provided a
very interesting and popular focal point for the reinterpretation of Puritanism in the post–Civil War period. The desire to believe, with the 1832
North American Review critic of Charles Upham's *Lectures on Witchcraft*, that "the progress of reason and knowledge" had put an end to such
superstitions as belief in witches was even stronger after the war than
before.[26] But the interest in the supernatural that accompanied Transcendentalism, the rise of spiritualism during the 1850s and 1860s, the wartime hysteria about Puritan witch hunters fanned by southerners and
Peace Democrats, and the popular flirtation with the occult arts during
the 1880s and 1890s, served as a painful reminder that superstition was
alive and well in nineteenth-century America. An outpouring of imaginative works on New England witchcraft before the war and the publication of three new historical studies immediately after, together with the
bicentennial of the Salem witchcraft trials in 1892, heightened sensitivity
to the relationship between Puritanism and superstition.[27] In terms of the
volume and intensity of discussion as well as its relevance to the historiographical theme of America's liberation from Puritan institutions, the
issue of witchcraft played almost as important a role in postbellum interpretations of Puritanism as the origins of American republicanism had

[25] Edward Eggleston, *The Beginners of a Nation* (New York: D. Appleton, 1897),
255–56, 267, 290, 306.

[26] Review of Charles Upham's *Lectures on Witchcraft*, in *NAR* 34 (January 1832):
219–20.

[27] In addition to Hawthorne's *The House of the Seven Gables* (1851), which dealt only
indirectly with the phenomenon of witchcraft, at least eight fictional works of note were
published between Upham's *Lectures* and W. Elliott Woodward's printing of the tran-
scripts of the Salem trial in 1864: William Leslie Stone, *Mercy Disborough: A Tale of
Witches* (1834); Eliza Buckminster Lee, *Delusion, of the Witch of New England* (1840);
the anonymous *The Salem Belle, A Tale of 1692* (1842); Benjamin Barker, *Zoraida or the
Witch of Naumkeag* (1845); H. W. Herbert, *The Innocent Witch* (1845); James Kirke
Paulding, *The Puritan and His Daughter* (1849); Cornelius Matthews, "Witchcraft, A
Tragedy in Five Acts" (1852); and John W. DeForest, "Witching Times," serialized in
Putnam's Magazine (1856–7). The postwar historical treatments were Samuel G. Drake,
The Salem Witchcraft Delusion in New England (1866), Charles Upham and Sons,
Salem Witchcraft (1867), and Drake, *Annals of Witchcraft in New England* (1869).

played in antebellum interpretations.

Of the three histories of New England witchcraft published in the late 1860s, Charles Upham's *Salem Witchcraft*, a follow-up to his earlier *Lectures*, received the most critical acclaim.[28] Like the filio-pietists' treatment of dissent, Upham's explanation of the witchcraft trials tried to reconstruct the seventeenth-century atmosphere in which they occurred. But his repeated emphasis on the contemporaneous decline of faith and ecclesiastical authority in colonial New England, and his demonstration that opposition to the persecution of alleged witches came from the people rather than from their leaders, anticipated the later reinterpretation of Puritan history. Upham's most scathing critic, William Frederick Poole, tried to prevent acceptance of a conspiratorial view of the Salem trials, objecting that since Upham's *Lectures*, Americans had learned that "nineteen innocent persons were hanged, and one was pressed to death, to gratify the vanity, ambition, and stolid credulity of Mr. Cotton Mather." A more accurate portrayal of the episode, including Mather's marginal role, Poole believed, appeared in Henry Wadsworth Longfellow's recent dramatic poem "Giles Corey of the Salem Farms."[29] But as Chadwick Hansen has pointed out, Poole's "strongest appeals were to ancestral piety and clerical solidarity," both of which were increasingly unacceptable motives for writing history.[30] As a consequence, even such traditional historians as Palfrey and Fiske devoted much of their treatments of witchcraft to rationalizing the clergy's persistent belief that the Devil was at work in New England.

In *The Emancipation of Massachusetts*, Brooks Adams sharpened Upham's conclusions, insuring that the bicentennial reexamination of the Salem witchcraft episode would focus more on the presumption of a clerical conspiracy to thwart spiritual freedom than on the conviction of the presence of evil spirits. Adams leveled all his guns at Cotton Mather, convinced that "it is not credible that an educated and sane man could ever have honestly believed in the absurd stuff which he produced as evidence of the supernatural." Adams was particularly galled that "Mather prided himself on what he had done," in part because the actions of the trial court had "left a stain upon the judiciary of Massachusetts that can never be effaced." Adams gained some consolation, however, from the fact that the appearance of Mather's *More Wonders of the Invisible World* in 1693, justifying the sentences handed down by the court, "may be said to mark an era in the intellectual development of Massachusetts, for it shook to its center the moral despotism which the

---

[28] Reviews of Charles Upham's *Salem Witchcraft*, in *Nation* 5 (November 14, 1867): 391, and *NAR* 106 (January 1868): 226, 230–31.

[29] William Frederick Poole, "Cotton Mather and Salem Witchcraft," *NAR* 108 (April 1869): 338, 395.

[30] Chadwick Hansen, *Witchcraft at Salem* (New York: George Braziller, 1969), xii.

pastors still kept almost unimpaired over the minds of their congrega-
tions, by demonstrating to the people the necessity of thinking for
themselves."[31]

The appearance in the early 1890s of Abijah Marvin's *The Life and
Times of Cotton Mather* and Barrett Wendell's *Cotton Mather, The
Puritan Priest* worried a literary critic for the *Nation* that "the name of
Mather is yet, and seems doomed to remain, fast associated" with the
1692 events in Salem the biographies commemorated.[32] Both works did
try to clear away some of the aspersions on Mather's reputation, marking
at least a partial triumph for William Poole's criticism of Salem witchcraft historiography. More significant for the historiography of the Puritan tradition as a whole, however, was the equation of perversion with
late seventeenth-century Puritanism that a more even-handed treatment
of Mather still could not challenge. This is especially apparent in a
pointed summary of his research that Wendell delivered to the Essex
Institute in Salem in 1892. His answer to the question "Were the Salem
Witches Guiltless?" indicates how even the most sympathetic student of
Puritanism could no longer ignore the evidence that Puritan society was
sick enough by the 1690s to breed conspiracy and contained a germ of
superstition virulent enough to infect American development.

Wendell subjected himself to occult experiences in order to try to
understand the "epidemic" that broke out in Salem in 1692. His own
psychological responses, together with his profound insight into the colonial Puritan belief in the supernatural, led him to conclude that

> whoever would understand the society from whose midst sprang the
> witches and the witch judges of 1692 must never forget the grim
> creed which, declaring that no man could be saved but by the special
> grace of God, and that the only test of salvation was ability to exert
> the will in accordance with His, bred in their counsels, an habitual
> introspection, and an habitual straining for mystical intercourse with
> the spiritual world, today almost inconceivable. In a world domina-
> ted by a creed at once so despairing and so mystic, it would not have
> been strange if now and then wretched men, finding in their endless
> introspection no sign of the divine marks of grace, and stimulated in
> their mysticism beyond modern conception by the churches that
> claimed and imposed an authority almost unsurpassed in history, had
> been tempted to seek, in premature alliance with the powers of evil,
> at least some semblance of the freedom that their inexorable God
> had denied them.

Here Wendell interpreted the witchcraft episode not as a conspiracy of
the Puritan elite against an incipient democracy, as did Brooks Adams,

[31] Brooks Adams, *Emancipation of Massachusetts*, 222, 225, 232, 236.

[32] Lindsay Swift review of Barrett Wendell's *Cotton Mather, The Puritan Priest* and
Abijah Marvin's *The Life and Times of Cotton Mather*, in *Nation* 55 (December 1,
1892): 414.

but as a conspiracy nonetheless. Agreeing with Adams that Puritanism had, at best, a precarious hold on New England society by the 1690s, Wendell portrayed the rumblings from below as a conspiracy of the nonelect who willingly placed themselves in the service of the Devil. Elsewhere in "Were the Salem Witches Guiltless?" Wendell speculated that, had not the trials of these conspirators surrounded the subject of witchcraft "with horror" prior to the "formative period of our national life," the rise of modern spiritualism, "followed by the excessive interest in occult matters so notable in the last ten years . . . might gravely have demoralized our national character." Lacking the Adamses' confidence in the progressive liberation of the human spirit, Wendell nonetheless followed their diagnosis of Puritanism diseased to the conclusion that the Puritan tradition transmitted to the United States a dark obsession with the supernatural.[33]

Puritan History Severed from Genteel Idealism

By the beginning of the twentieth century Barrett Wendell had cast his lot with the literary historians whose specialization came to include what once had been of interest to all American historians, the fate of Puritan ideals and principles. Colonial historians, influenced by Herbert Baxter Adams's new institutional approach, increasingly ignored the cultural and social questions that, to varying degrees, historians still asked during the early postbellum period. In fact, they displayed little interest in Puritanism as a movement at all. In his local studies *River Towns of Connecticut* and *Colonial Self-Government 1625–1659*, Charles McLean Andrews generally neglected the Puritan ideal of the Christian Commonwealth and the impact of changes in political structure on that ideal. Herbert Osgood's *The American Colonies in the Seventeenth Century* included a thorough institutional analysis of the relation between church and state in New England but uncritically followed Brooks and Charles Francis Adams's accounts of the Puritan treatment of dissent.[34] And although his work covered the Phips administration under the Charter of 1691, Osgood made no mention of the witchcraft episode in Salem. Edward Channing's *A History of the United States* was, by comparison, more attentive to the character and history of Puritanism, but the very matter-of-factness of his presentation indicated how thoroughly the Puritan tradition had been demythologized.

The detached tone of Channing's interpretations of the Puritan legacy, dissent, and witchcraft veils only superficially the modern historian's

[33] Barrett Wendell, "Were the Salem Witches Guiltless?" *Stelligeri and Other Essays Concerning America* (New York: Scribner's, 1893), 89, 101.
[34] Herbert L. Osgood, *The American Colonies in the Seventeenth Century* (New York: Columbia Univ. Press, 1904–07), vols. I and III.

struggle to represent Puritanism "without caricature or repugnance," once the Puritans' self-appraisal received critical scrutiny. Channing's description of the Puritan spirit is traditional enough in content to make the shallowness of its understanding transparent.

> Seventeenth-century Puritanism was an attitude of mind rather than a system of theology,—it was idealism applied to the solution of contemporary problems. In religion it took the form of a demand for preaching ministers and for carrying to its logical ending the reformation in the ecclesiastical fabric which Elizabeth had begun and had stopped halfway. In society it assumed the shape of a desire to elevate private morals, which were shockingly low. In politics it stood for a new movement in national life, which required the extirpation of the relics of feudalism and the recognition of the people as a power in the State. In short, Puritanism marked the beginning of the rising tide of human aspiration for something better than the world had yet known.

Channing apparently believed that Roger Williams's protests in favor of the separation of church and state were much ado about nothing because "politics and religion were then so closely interwoven that neither the participants nor ourselves can disentangle them." And his explanation of the Salem witchcraft phenomenon is so understated that caricature must have been especially tempting: "There can be no doubt that in the course of these persecutions the charge of witchcraft was used for purposes of private revenge and also to get rid of unpopular persons. On the other hand, some of those who were condemned had doubtless employed mental suggestion or hypnosis to worry those whom they disliked." Channing's judgments do not lack integrity; indeed they are moderate and balanced. But against the background of the rewriting of Puritan history in the postbellum period, their very moderation and balance betray the strain of trying to be objective about colonial New England's contribution to American development.[35]

America's postbellum historians failed to achieve objectivity toward Puritanism, although they may have thought they did. Instead, the legacy of self-government was now discovered in rebellion against, rather than in the providential transformation of, Puritan theocracy; the suppression of dissent in colonial New England was highlighted, and the dissenters became heroes and heroines rather than merely footnotes; and the witchcraft episode revealed a peculiarly New England Puritan psychosis rather than a relatively common early modern Christian purge of evil. Several succeeding generations of professional historians have yet to resolve these complex issues in the historiography of Puritanism, but the impact of the first generation's recognition of them is what matters here.

[35] Edward Channing, A History of the United States, 2 vols. (New York: Macmillan, 1905) I: 368–69, 461–62.

It is impossible to say whether the history of American Puritanism would have been treated so critically, especially by New England's own sons, had the disillusioning Civil War experience alone informed their historical judgment. But reinforced by the search for rational laws of historical development and by secular scholarship's aversion to religion, supernaturalism, and high idealism, that experience made it difficult to find much to praise in Puritanism and very little to link Puritan history to either the emerging genteel tradition or the contemporaneous search of American literati for artistic inspiration.

8

The Puritan Artist as Solitary Seeker

In 1906, the same year in which Theodore Clark Smith confessed that the twentieth-century historical imagination had difficulty representing the colonial Puritan mind without caricature or repugnance, the *North American Review* published Henry James's essay "Boston" in which he confessed that the creative imagination also had difficulty receiving sustenance from the Puritan tradition. James summarized the concern of literary artists and critics during most of the post–Civil War period as he pondered "of what the old New England spirit may have still, intellectually, aesthetically, or for that matter, even morally, to give; of what may yet remain, for productive scraping, of the formula of the native Puritan educated, the formula once capacious enough for the 'literary constellation' of the Age of Emerson."[1] The postbellum man of letters, like the historian, believed that the Age of Emerson had captured the Puritan spirit with special insight; but whereas Charles Francis Adams, Jr., might welcome Hawthorne's *Twice-Told Tales* as a complement to his own effort to reconstruct the past, the man of letters often despaired of erecting a culture on a tradition so seemingly out of tune with the present. After the death of Emerson in 1882, American literati hastened to reexamine their inheritance from Puritanism in the light of a generational crisis William Dean Howells could still poignantly describe in 1901:

> The New England poets and essayists and historians who gave Boston its primacy, are in that moment of their abeyance when the dead are no longer felt as contemporaries, and are not yet established as classics. It is the moment of misgiving, or of worse, concerning them; and it is altogether natural that this doubt should be most felt where their past greatness was most felt.[2]

The understanding of Puritanism that emerged from this crisis eventually darkened educated attitudes toward the Puritan tradition even more than the revisionism of the historian by calling more seriously into question the utility of Puritanism in a new age.

---

[1] Henry James, "Boston," *NAR* 182 (March 1906): 344–45.
[2] William Dean Howells, "Professor Barrett Wendell's Notions of American Literature," *NAR* 172 (April 1901): 624.

At stake in the crisis were the conflicting needs, on one hand, of affirming that the United States had a distinctive national culture that had reached maturity during the Age of Emerson and, on the other, of denying that the subjectivism and regional chauvinism of the period of maturation were necessarily the representative expression of that culture. In other words, Puritanism had made its most significant contribution to the development of American culture in the work of Emerson and his contemporaries; but the culture produced by the Emersonian circle was only one, and even a rather primitive, stage of American civilization needing to continue its development but presently lacking inspiration.

The process of affirmation began immediately after the Civil War and lasted through the aftermath of the shock of Emerson's passing in 1882. It responded to the publication of the English critic Matthew Arnold's *Culture and Anarchy* and the retrospective mood accompanying the celebration of the national centennial. Moses Coit Tyler's *History of American Literature* molded its historical perspective and Henry James's *Hawthorne, English Men of Letters* offered a timely reflection on the relation between Puritanism and the individual creative genius.

The process of denial began with Emerson's death and Matthew Arnold's 1883–84 United States lecture tour. The work of Edmund Stedman, George Woodberry, and Barrett Wendell molded its historical perspective and Paul Elmer More's 1901 *Atlantic* article "The Solitude of Nathaniel Hawthorne" marked the critical distance traveled from James's *Hawthorne*. In the transition from affirmation to denial, Puritanism ceased being a religious tradition elevating the artistic spirit and became instead an ethical tradition obsessed with the moral isolation of the individual. At odds with the socialization of morality attending the rise of social criticism and the Social Gospel at the end of the nineteenth century, the New England artist's sense of moral isolation readily became the focal point for criticizing the nation's cultural inheritance from Puritanism. Thus, the final resolution of the generational crisis experienced by James and Howells was the admission that the "Puritan self" of the Emersonian circle was unequal to the task of reconciling art and life, individual and society, national character and national culture in the modern age.[3]

----

[3] Although it does not examine the postbellum period, Sacvan Bercovitch's *Puritan Origins of the American Self* suggests a useful perspective on the literary criticism of the period. Thomas Hartshorne's *The Distorted Image: Changing Conceptions of the American Character Since Turner* (Cleveland, Ohio: Press of Case Western Reserve University, 1968) discusses the relationship between Puritanism and the search for a national identity in the twentieth century.

Emerson, Affirmation of the Puritan Self, and the Rebuttal to Matthew Arnold

The literary critics and historians of post–Civil War America inherited from such romantic commentators as Henry Tuckerman some concern about the shallowness of the Puritan aesthetic sense. They were also confronted with rebellion against convention heralded by the publication of Walt Whitman's *Leaves of Grass* in 1855. But more urgent to most than either of these issues immediately following the war was defending the integrity of American culture, and especially its Puritan roots, from the English critic Matthew Arnold. Arnold's analysis of the cultural ramifications of established versus nonconformist religion sounded too much like the South's expose of the secularization of Puritan orthodoxy to ignore. In the preface to *Culture and Anarchy*, Arnold linked the exclusive preoccupation of the Puritan with religious matters to a one dimensional national life that, in Arnold's terms, hardly even deserved the label culture. To Arnold, genuine culture was the common possession of an entire people, allowing those among the mass who are so inclined to perfect all sides of their individual characters equally. It gives "a sense of the historical life of the human spirit outside and beyond our own fancies and feelings." The absence of genuine culture is both caused by, and in turn stimulates, "the condition of self-assertion and challenge" that the individual Puritan chooses for himself. The resulting absence of the "leisure and calm," essential to the creation and enjoyment of true culture, ultimately, inhibits the full development of even man's religious side: "in a serious people [such as the Americans], where every one has to choose and strive for his own order and discipline of religion, the contention about non-essentials occupies his mind." Whatever "crude notions" the individual first has about religion "do not get purged"; and, in a powerful image adumbrating later American criticism of the Puritan artist, Arnold concluded that these notions "invade the whole spiritual man" and there make "a solitude." Thus, the character of the solitary seekers in a Puritan nation can conceive a national life distinguished only by provincialism, a provincialism not so much of locale or class but finally of individual isolation.[4]

Thomas Higginson's January 1870 *Atlantic* article "Americanism in Literature" refuted Arnold by making a positive case for the Puritan origins of a genuine national culture in the United States, soon seconded by Edwin Whipple and Moses Coit Tyler, among others. America's past cultural accomplishments and future cultural potential were located, they contended, in the religious tradition of New England Puritanism, characterized not by provincialism but by "its enthusiasm and its

---

[4] *Culture and Anarchy*, in *The Complete Prose Works of Matthew Arnold*, ed. R. H. Super (Ann Arbor: Univ. of Michigan Press, 1965) V: 239, 243–45.

truthfulness."[5] The source of its enthusiasm was the Calvinist doctrine of grace, or direct communication between God and the human soul, and it gave American culture a peculiar depth of spiritual insight associated with Jonathan Edwards's experience of "the most enrapturing visions of the spiritual joy of heaven" and the "passionate" zeal and "glowing heart" of all the Puritans' ancestors.[6] The source of its truthfulness was the existence in New England of, in Tyler's words, a "thinking community" wherein reasoning and feeling combined to form the integrity of character which "not only dared to have ideas, but dared to put them together and face the logical consequences of them." Even though, according to Tyler,

> the aesthetic sense was crushed down and almost trampled out by the felt tyranny of their creed . . . in pure and wholesome natures such as theirs, its emergence was only a matter of normal growth. They who have their eyes fixed in adoration upon the beauty of holiness, are not far from the sight of all beauty. It is not permitted us to doubt that in music, in painting, architecture, sculpture, poetry, prose, the highest art will be reached in some epoch of its growth by the robust and versatile race sprung from those practical idealists of the seventeenth century—those impassioned seekers after the invisible truth and beauty and goodness.[7]

Taking their lead from the literary historians' affirmation of the potential vitality of Puritan culture, literary critics looked to Ralph Waldo Emerson as the nineteenth-century prophet of the spiritual enrichment of New England's religious tradition. To some of his contemporaries Emerson represented, to others he prefigured, the capacity of all Americans to achieve spiritual freedom through the self-ordering of the soul in a union of the human and the divine wills. The identity of religious character and national culture in the literary productions of Emerson and his circle sustained the belief that the Puritan self, as America's, could achieve salvation through perfection. And it was Matthew Arnold who preached that the achievement of salvation through perfection was the final test and goal of genuine culture.[8]

[5] Thomas Higginson, "Americanism in Literature," *Atlantic* 25 (January 1870): 60.

[6] Edwin Whipple, "American Literature," *Harper's* 52 (February 1876): 402, and Moses Coit Tyler, *History of American Literature, 1607–1765* (New York: Collier Books, 1962), 111.

[7] Tyler, *History of American Literature*, 109, 121. For similar sentiments see "The First Century of the Republic, Introduction: Our Colonial Progress," *Harper's* 69 (November 1874): 865–78; Edwin Whipple, "American Literature, Part II," *Harper's* 52 (March 1876): 517–28; John Chadwick, "In Western Massachusetts," *Harper's* 56 (November 1880): 874.

[8] See the following commentaries on Emerson: Review of Thoreau's *Letters to Various Persons*, in *NAR* 101 (October 1867): 599; Francis H. Underwood, "Ralph Waldo Emerson," *NAR* 130 (May 1880): 486; Julian Hawthorne, "Ralph Waldo Emerson," *Harper's* 65 (July

Emerson and his generation were not without their early critics, however, even before the mid-1880s. Julian Ward explicitly, and F. G. Ireland implicitly, questioned whether the apotheosis of spirituality in the character of the individual Transcendentalist provided a sufficient foundation for national culture. And both echoed Arnoldian suspicions of the provincialism of a culture grounded in Puritan religion. In "The Decay of New England Thought" Ward noted that Transcendentalism had not solved the problem of America's need for a "catholic belief" like the Roman or Anglican any better than colonial Puritanism. Transcendentalism had, according to Ward, only partially absorbed the modern conviction that "the personality of God is the ground work for the personality of man" and thus had failed to synthesize Puritanism and democracy into a native Christian humanism more Christian than Arnold's humanism and more collectivist than Emersonian individualism.[9] Ireland, too, despaired of uniting the benign influence of democracy with Puritanism and sharply indicted Transcendental spiritual elitism. "When a man seeks to break the bonds of Puritanism," he wrote, "to burst forth from the prison where our spirit has lain for two hundred years enchained, he almost invariably becomes an iconoclast, a radical by profession,—not for truth's sake but for radicalism's sake."[10] From somewhat different perspectives, Ward and Ireland both questioned the representative character of the Transcendentalist prophet, holding that his brand of individualism was anachronistic; and in so doing, they also prophetically questioned his fitness to be a purveyor of the national culture.

Henry James's essay on Hawthorne in *English Men of Letters* also raised, indirectly, the problem of the relation among the Puritan tradition, individualism, and society, while still affirming the potential vitality of Puritan culture. James identified the Puritan tradition inherited by Hawthorne with its "dusky, overshadowed conscience." Contrary to prevailing opinion, however, James asserted that Hawthorne had not internalized the Puritan conscience either as a basis for his own moral outlook or as a theological belief. Reluctant to reduce the Puritan legacy to moralism, James argued that Hawthorne had an intellectual rather than a moralistic awareness of the existence of the ancestral, Puritan sense of sin, and in it Hawthorne's unique imaginative genius was able to discover a universal

1882): 279–81; William T. Harris, "Ralph Waldo Emerson," *Atlantic* 50 (August 1882): 239; Edwin Whipple, "Some Recollections of Ralph Waldo Emerson," *Harper's* 65 (September 1882): 576–87; George Bancroft, "Holmes' *Life of Emerson*," NAR 140 (February 1886): 133; review by Horace Scudder, *Atlantic* 60 (October 1887): 569. For Matthew Arnold's influential definition of genuine culture see *Culture and Anarchy*, 243.

9 Julian H. Ward, "The Decay of New England Thought," NAR 133 (September 1881): 277.

10 F. G. Ireland, "Puritanism and Manners," *Atlantic* 43 (February 1879): 163. Both Ward and Ireland evidence familiarity with Arnold's essay, "Equality," in *Essays Religious and Mixed*, in *The Complete Prose Works of Matthew Arnold*, VIII: 277–305.

human secret: "When he was most creative, the moral picturesqueness of the old secret of mankind in general and of the Puritans in particular, most appealed to him—the secret that we are really not by any means so good as a well-regulated society requires us to appear." Thus, like other representatives of the genteel tradition, James affirmed that Puritanism could still enrich the national culture through its own substantive conceptions of reality. Freed of dogma like the Transcendentalist experience of spirituality but, in contrast to Transcendentalism, illuminating the essence of social rather than individual reality, Hawthorne's Puritan sense of sin had done precisely that. In fact, the most significant difference between James's 1879 analysis of Hawthorne and those written at the turn of the century was that James believed Hawthorne had understood social reality correctly and later critics did not. James credited Hawthorne with translating one of the most narrow aspects of the national character, the Puritan sense of sin, into the kind of universal insight which informs genuine culture. By the turn of the century, however, critics more often accused Hawthorne of contributing to the provincialism of national culture because of his preoccupation with individual conscience.[11]

Hawthorne, Condemnation of the Puritan Self, and the Rise of Social Consciousness

James's insight that Hawthorne had discovered a universal secret in Puritan spirituality was reflected after the mid-1880s in the literary historians' search for other examples of the Puritan grasp of reality. Whereas Whipple's and Tyler's histories had established a link between Puritan religion and the creation of an atmosphere in which culture could flourish, literary histories by Stedman, Woodberry, and Wendell evaluated Puritan literature in terms of whether its portrayal of reality presently appeared to be true or false. But whereas the literary historians Stedman, Woodberry, and Wendell generally agreed on the truth of that portrayal, late nineteenth-century literary critics became convinced of the falsity of the Puritan view of reality appropriated by the Age of Emerson.

When William Dean Howells reviewed the first three volumes of the *Library of American Literature*, compiled by Stedman and E. M. Hutchinson, he was careful to note the sustaining appeal of Puritan letters: Roger Williams's impassioned defense of toleration in *The Bloody Tenent yet More Bloody*, spoke directly to a people "who have accepted toleration rather with their tongues than with their hearts"; Michael

---

[11] Henry James, *Hawthorne, English Men of Letters* (New York: Harper & Bros., 1894), XIII: 56, 99. Not far removed from James's interpretation was E. P. Peabody, "The Genius of Hawthorne," *Atlantic* 22 (September 1868): 359–74. The American disciple of Matthew Arnold, W. C. Brownell, placed James's interpretation in perspective in a review in *Nation* 30 (January 29, 1880): 80–81.

Wigglesworth's *The Day of Doom* was of a genre among the most moving in literature, "full of dark fascination which every reader of aesthetic sensibility must recognize"; and even though Cotton Mather's "Wonder-Working Providence" marked a "moral and intellectual lapse of New England" society, "modern spiritualism . . . has never expressed itself so attractively."[12] In 1903, the same year in which he published *America in Literature*, George Woodberry traced in an article in *Harper's* the spirituality that "underlies [New England's] historic democracy as the things of eternity underlie the things of time." This spirituality culminated in the work of Emerson who "kept the old perspective of the relative worth of spiritual and temporal things inherited from Puritan days in the habits of mind, and held to the lasting transcendency of the one and the evanescence of the other."[13] The most influential and controversial of the new literary historians, Barrett Wendell, celebrated the quest for absolute truth expressed in the "strenuously self-searching inner life" of New England in *A Literary History of America*. This quest, sometimes misconceived as mere idealism, was in reality "a profound and lasting spiritual power" that outlived the decline of the church into formalism at the end of the seventeenth century and the "mad shoutings and tearing off of garments" associated with the piety of eighteenth century revivalism. During the Revolutionary era, the Puritan search for truth settled on "an instinctive liking for absolute right," and still later the Transcendentalists concentrated "their whole temperamental energy in efforts definitely to perceive absolute truths quite beyond the range of earthly sense."[14] In terms of its general, historical influence, then, the Puritan tradition had provided Americans with insight into the political, spiritual, and moral truths that all genuine culture seeks to illuminate.

The literary critics after the mid-1880s, in contrast to these literary historians, were dissatisfied with the results of the Puritan quest for truth. Soon after Emerson's death, American critics became impatient to go beyond the work of the man whom Howells called the "consummate flower of Puritanism."[15] While Matthew Arnold was mellowing in his evaluation of Puritanism, remarking on his American lecture tour of 1883–84 that "the more I read history, the more I see of mankind, the more I recognize its value,"[16] his American admirers increasingly shared the despair of F. G. Ireland that the United States has "no past, no national tradition, no

[12] Editor's Study, *Harper's* 77 (August 1888): 477–79.

[13] George Woodberry, "The Literary Age of Boston," *Harper's* 106 (February 1903): 426–27.

[14] Barrett Wendell, *A Literary History of America* (New York: Scribner's, 1900): 70, 75, 238, 241, 293–94.

[15] Editor's Study, *Harper's* 76 (April 1888): 805.

[16] Matthew Arnold, "Numbers," *Philistinism in England and New England*, in *Complete Prose Works*, X: 164.

history" to which the creative spirit could appeal other than Puritanism.[17] And as if self-consciously wielding Arnold's own weapons against his most recent conclusions, they set out to discredit the Age of Emerson and its residual Puritanism by exposing the weaknesses of the Emersonian character and their destructive effect in American literature.

Two qualities of the Emersonian character, and of the style derived from it, received severe condemnation from late nineteenth-century critics, moralism and insubstantiality. Howells's commentary gave especially vivid expression to both. He described the works of Lowell, Holmes, Whittier, Hawthorne, and Emerson as the "Socinian [that is, rationalistic] graft of a Calvinist stock": "Their faith, in its various shades and colors, was Unitarian, but their art was Puritan . . . marred by the intense ethicism that pervaded the New England mind for two hundred years."[18] Like Howells, the critic and poet John Jay Chapman emphasized that, although the Emersonians were free of theological dogma, they came "very near being dogmatic in their reiteration of the Moral Law."[19] Furthermore, Emerson and the other Transcendentalists had surrounded themselves with an aura of abstractness. Howells recounted the following impression from his first trip from Ohio to New England to document his claim that New England Puritanism continued to create "colorless rigidities," even in the Age of Emerson:

> I do not remember that Thoreau spoke of his books or of himself at all, and when he began to speak of John Brown it was not the warm, palpable, loving, fearful old man of my conception, but a sort of John Brown type, a John Brown ideal, a John Brown principle, which we were somehow (with long pauses, between the vague, orphic phrases) to cherish and to nourish ourselves upon. . . . When I came away it was with the feeling that there was very little more left of John Brown than there was of me. His body was not mouldering in the grave, neither was his soul marching; his ideal, his type, his principle alone existed; and I did not know what to do with it.

Elsewhere Howells wrote of Emerson's Puritanism: "He was so much an idealization of the ordinary human being that his fears are attenuated, like his sympathies."[20]

John Jay Chapman linked the qualities of moralism and insubstantiality together in explaining how "conscience may destroy character." Lack of emotional depth among the Emersonians resulted, Chapman

---

[17] Ireland, "Puritanism and Manners," 163.

[18] William Dean Howells, "Literary Boston Thirty Years Ago," *Harper's* 91 (November 1895): 868–69.

[19] John Jay Chapman, "Emerson Sixty Years Ago," *Atlantic* 79 (February 1897): 225–26.

[20] Howells, "Literary Boston," 874; William Dean Howells, "My First Visit to New England," *Harper's* 89 (August 1894): 447–48; Editor's Study, *Harper's* 76 (February 1888): 477.

claimed, from the distrust or repression of forms of desire for the good and the just other than those dictated by conscience. "This anaemic incompleteness of . . . character can be traced to the philosophy of the race. . . . There is an implication of a fundamental falsehood in every bit of Transcendentalism, including Emerson. That falsehood consists in the theory of the self-sufficiency of each individual, men and women, alike." In other words, not only did the New England mind suffer from a preoccupation with the ideal of life rather than life itself; each individual mind entertained its own ideal in isolation.[21]

In "The Solitude of Nathaniel Hawthorne," accordingly, Paul Elmer More portrayed Hawthorne as a prophet of escape from the false theory of the self-sufficiency of the individual. The theme of Hawthorne's work, wrote More, was "the penalty of solitude laid upon the human soul" when it turns inward toward the self rather than outward toward the common life of humanity. From Jonathan Edwards, the New England mind inherited the belief that "the moral governance of the world revolved about the action of each mortal soul," and the Transcendentalists carried the associated habit of introspection to an extreme. Hawthorne himself was not immune to the disease of introspection but, according to More, Hawthorne's loss of faith in the ever-present reality of God left him with a moral sense of the "infinite isolation of the errant soul." Therefore, Hawthorne portrayed both evil—solitude—and its retribution—greater solitude—as one and the same. But even more importantly, he broke through this cycle to reveal the truth that the only salvation from evil and its retribution is the renunciation of the self.[22]

The year following the publication of More's article in 1901, Howells applauded Hawthorne's *The Scarlet Letter* for teaching the lesson that "a sin owned is a sin put away." It is not difficult to read Howells's words as a metaphor of the task with which he believed Hawthorne had confronted the American artist who, for too long, had isolated himself from the mainstream of national life by failing "to grasp the difference between wrong and evil . . . as the means of rendering life truly."[23] Harsher critics than More and Howells, on the other hand, interpreted Hawthorne's life and works as symptomatic of that very problem. When

---

[21] Chapman, "Emerson Sixty Years Ago," 229. Also see Editor's Easy Chair, *Harper's* 68 (December 1883): 149; Walt Whitman, "Have We a National Literature?" *NAR* 152 (March 1891): 335–36; Gamaliel Bradford, Jr., "The American Idealist," *Atlantic* 70 (July 1892): 88; George William Curtis, "Oliver Wendell Holmes," *Harper's* 83 (July 1891): 280; and the following articles on James Russell Lowell: F. H. Underwood, *Harper's* 72 (January 1881): 252–73; Henry James, *Atlantic* 69 (January 1892): 35–50; and Charles Eliot Norton, *Harper's* 86 (May 1893): 846–57.

[22] Paul Elmer More, "The Solitude of Nathaniel Hawthorne," *Atlantic* 88 (November 1901): 590, 592, 597, 598.

[23] Editor's Easy Chair, *Harper's* 105 (November 1902): 967.

Annie Logan reviewed George Woodberry's *Nathaniel Hawthorne* in 1902, she found its major theme to be Hawthorne's inability to dissociate himself from "an intense self-consciousness of life in the soul." Hawthorne's principal concern, she affirmed, was the secret sin that, more than any other, separated men from God and from honest relations with each other.[24] Hamilton Wright Mabie recalled that one of the prominent features of Hawthorne's life was his separation from his family: "The emphasis on personality, which was the note of the Puritan view of life and the source of its strength and weakness, had produced a peculiar type of morbid character in New England, the distinguishing mark of which is its passion for solitude." "Hawthorne's Puritan inheritance," Mabie continued, "showed itself in his absorption in the problems not only of the spirit, but of the spirit out of harmony with itself and at odds with its own nature."[25] Theodore Munger simply described Hawthorne's concept of sin in *The Scarlet Letter* as that which "separates man from God and his fellows, and at last from himself."[26]

These critics of Hawthorne saw the central problem of America's Puritan culture as a preoccupation with the self, meaning not self-indulgence but the inability to treat reality other than the self as the proper subject for the creative imagination. American literature, according to these commentators, could not deal creatively with the relation of the self to the world. Under the influence of Puritanism, American authors perceived the self and the world in opposition to one another. But they lacked the imagination to construct a link between the self and the world or even to deal with the self–world conflict as a challenge to artistic creativity. Instead, American authors viewed external reality as a kind of intrusion on the moral integrity of the self, a moral integrity they were determined at all costs to preserve. To critics of American Puritan culture an integrity isolating the creative imagination from the world outside the self was not, in James Huneker's words, "morality, but a psychic disorder."[27] Instead of moral integrity, the legacy of Puritanism was narcissism.

Huneker was the godfather of those early twentieth-century Puritan-baiters, like H. L. Mencken, who believed Puritanism represented American culture and society diseased, but he also echoed the older generation of historians who identified Puritans with pathology. Theirs was an extreme

24 Annie Logan quoting from George Woodberry's *Nathaniel Hawthorne*, in *Nation* 75 (December 11, 1902): 464.

25 Hamilton Wright Mabie, "Nathaniel Hawthorne," *NAR* 179 (July 1904): 18–19.

26 Theodore Munger, "Notes on The Scarlet Letter," *Atlantic* 93 (April 1904): 530. Henry G. Fairbanks's *The Lasting Loneliness of Nathaniel Hawthorne: A Study in the Sources of Alienation in Modern Man* (Albany, N.Y.: Magi Books, 1965), is an interesting recent analysis along similar lines.

27 James Huneker review in *NAR* 185 (June 7, 1907): 336–37.

view, although thanks to the prolific Mencken, better known then and today than George Santayana's more measured portrayal of the genteel tradition as American culture and society merely debilitated. In both forms, however, the early twentieth-century preoccupation with exposing, and finally purging, the United States of its veneration for Puritanism was profoundly indebted to the generational crisis endured by Henry James and William Dean Howells. They had been the first heirs of Puritan New England culture to receive little stimulation from the Puritan impulse and to take little nourishment from Puritan truths. Unlike their contemporaries in New England's Protestant establishment, it was not enough for them to discover analogues between past and present attitudes, and to call the latter Puritan to invest them with the authority of tradition. Nor could they, the makers of culture, be quite as cavalier about dissecting a legacy as the writers of history. The civilization molded by Puritanism was the material of their art; the Age of Emerson was the American intellectuals' epiphany.

The inability of late nineteenth-century literati to gain strength from the Puritan struggle found its proper image in the isolated self. The younger generation was exploring the social and collective dimensions of national life, and the inward-looking, antisocial character of writers in the Puritan tradition was out of touch with their reality. Entertaining thoughts of America's newly acquired international responsibilities, the literati found nothing to admire in the provincialism of the solitary seeker. But at another level the isolated self was also the persona of the creative artist at the turn of the century, a projection of the intellectual severed from the only culture that, Matthew Arnold notwithstanding, deserved the label in the United States. The isolated self, the solitary seeker, represented not only the Emersonians consumed with Puritanism but also their sons and daughters consumed by Puritanism. The next generation, the grandsons and granddaughters of the Age of Emerson, would find images of Puritanism corresponding more closely to the larger social world in which they grew up, and they would use them to diagnose the illness not of the individual soul but of the soul of America.

9

Creating a Usable Past

In 1918 the young cultural critic Van Wyck Brooks wrote an essay for *Dial* entitled "On Creating a Usable Past," calling for the discovery and exploitation of American traditions suited to the dynamic, pluralistic society the United States had then become. Having become familiar, while at Harvard, with New England's recently demythologized past and with the soul-searching accompanying the death of Emerson, and provoked by the narrow patriotism of America's World War I propaganda effort, Brooks especially pressed for the creation of pasts other than the Puritan.[1] The historian Frederick Hoffman has, since his 1949 *American Quarterly* article, "Philistine and Puritan in the 1920's: An Example of the Misuse of the American Past," helped to immortalize Brooks's essay by using it as if it were a manifesto for the anti-Puritanism of the 1920s.[2] According to Hoffman, rather than creating usable pasts other than Puritanism, critics such as H. L. Mencken self-consciously created of Puritanism an unsympathetic caricature of the provincial, bourgeois America they so despised. At first holding this willfully distorted mirror up to American culture in the hope of shocking it into self-recognition, they later, in the words of a Brooks scholar influenced by Hoffman, discarded it "as a straw man," making the boisterous debate about Puritan influence on American civilization no more than another diversion for the era's Lost Generation.[3] It must be remembered, however, that not only Van Wyck Brooks but a number of his contemporary rebels, including Mencken, had been serious students of the Puritan tradition for at least a decade before the *Dial* article. The fact that their criticism of American culture, both before and after the war, focused on the Puritan, rather than on some other tradition, is an important commentary on the residual power of the Puritan legacy over their imaginations. They did not so much imagine a Puritan past purposefully at odds with the truth as graft their ambivalence toward the

---

[1] Van Wyck Brooks, "On Creating a Usable Past," in *Van Wyck Brooks: The Early Years*, ed. Claire Sprague (New York: Harper & Row, Harper Torchbook, 1968), 219–26.

[2] Frederick J. Hoffman, "Philistine and Puritan in the 1920's: An Example of the Misuse of the American Past," *American Quarterly* 1 (Fall 1949): 247–63. Also see Hoffman's *The Twenties* (New York: Macmillan, Free Press Paperback, 1965), 355–69.

[3] James R. Vitelli, *Van Wyck Brooks* (New York: Twayne, 1969), 65.

decline of Puritan spirituality onto the prevailing negative evaluations put
forward by historians and literary critics. If anything, the respect they
showed Puritanism by creating usable pasts only in dialectical relation to
the Puritan makes them the heirs rather than the destroyers of the
impulse behind the genteel tradition. And they did not so much toss the
issue of the Puritan past away after tiring of it as they sat by and watched
commentators favorably disposed toward Puritanism, in their anxiety to
preserve it, actually hasten making Puritanism unusable by completely
secularizing it.

Puritanism's Spiritual Hegemony and America's Spiritual Bankruptcy

The generation seeking to create pasts more usable than Puritanism
was the same generation Henry May says ended America's innocence
and Morton White says revolted against formalism.[4] Both moral innocence and intellectual formalism were blamed on the Puritan tradition:
moral isolation made for moral innocence, and the scholastic defense of
genteel idealism fostered formalism. When it came to creating usable
pasts, Puritanism was blamed for the, until very recently, uncontested
hegemony it had exercised over the nation's conception of its own identity. Even those who envisioned an America different from the Puritan
ideal had to do so in terms of escaping from or discarding the Puritan
legacy. Or so it seemed to a generation unable to measure its own aspirations for American culture and society except against the aspirations of
others who had acknowledged their debt to Puritanism and, unable to
find a language in which to couch its aspirations as resonant as the language of Puritanism long had been.

The rebellious generation spanning the war years experienced this
Puritan hegemony as a spiritual crisis, as an unnatural confinement of
the individual and communal imagination. And in order for them to
challenge that hegemony effectively and create for America more usable
pasts, they would have to derive from their spiritual crisis a new form of
historical consciousness. This experience was shared by those who struggled merely to rise up to meet Puritan standards as well as by those who
dreamed of rising up against them. America suffered, according to a
friendly reviewer of Van Wyck Brooks's anti-Puritan *Letters and Leadership* in 1918, from "spiritual deficiency." "All the younger generation,"
another commentator observed, "felt that America was too small to contain the spirit that would soar." Waldo Frank, in his important dissident
manifesto *Our America*, blamed "the Puritan philosophy" for preventing
the birth of "spiritual force" in the United States. Frank's diagnosis of

---

[4] Henry May, *The End of American Innocence* (Chicago: Quadrangle Paperbacks,
1964); Morton White, *Social Thought in America: The Revolt against Formalism* (Boston: Beacon Press, 1957).

the condition of the country, if not his explanation of the cause, was also accepted by admirers of Puritanism—it was a land presently "empty of spirit." One such admirer, Bliss Perry, bemoaned "the transition from the spiritual intensity of a few of our earlier writers to the sentimental qualities which have brought popular recognition to the many." Robert Lynd transformed Perry's complaint into "An Apology for Puritans" rebuking his generation's bohemianism with the reminder that "Puritanism is abstinence from the ecstasies of the sensations as a means of making possible the ecstasies of the spirit." And in 1936 Gilbert Seldes recalled his generation's spiritual backsliding by noting that Jonathan Edwards "writes of God with more ecstasy than any other American has expressed on any subject whatsoever."[5]

In the works and lives of two American literati other than Edwards, Nathaniel Hawthorne and Henry Adams, the young intellectuals of the early twentieth century found important and useful symbols of recurring spiritual crises in American history and their rather mysterious link to the Puritan tradition. What made these symbols especially appropriate was a certain "weird" quality, in the sense in which Paul Elmer More applied the term to Hawthorne's images: "not the veritable vision of unearthly things, but the peculiar half-vision inherited by the soul when faith has waned and the imagination prolongs the old sensations in a shadowy involuntary life of its own." Identification of their own spiritual bankruptcy with the spiritual bankruptcy of Hawthorne's and Adams's lifetimes became, in other words, a vehicle for describing the paradoxical attitude that eventually bred in the new generation a dialectical historical imagination. On one hand, they experienced Puritanism as an anachronism; but on the other, their perception of America's present spiritual deficiency supposed a standard of spiritual sufficiency, and if that standard existed anywhere in American culture, it was in the highest achievements of Puritanism itself. William MacDonald alluded to this paradox in his 1921 review of James Truslow Adams's highly critical The Founding of New England: "It is a relief to be assured that no such State as the Puritan colony of Massachusetts is sometimes represented to have been ever really existed. For . . . if Puritanism and sturdy virtue are in any degree synonymous, we must admit we ourselves are neither sturdy nor virtuous." And Benjamin DeCasseres, biographer of the first modern anti-Puritan James Huneker, accused the American intellectual as late as 1927 of not having "the courage to change" the Puritan "standard of Life and

5 Francis Hackett's review of Van Wyck Brooks's Letters and Leadership, in NR 16 (September 28, 1918): 261; Rose C. Field, "A Plea for Reticence," NR 36 (October 3, 1923): 153; Waldo Frank, Our America (New York: Boni & Liveright, 1919), 227; Bliss Perry, The American Mind (Port Washington, N.Y.: Kennikat Press, 1912), 110; Robert Lynd, "An Apology for the Puritans," Living Age 282 (July 11, 1914): 122; Gilbert Seldes, Mainland (New York: Scribner's, 1936), 65.

Morals" to which he is "the heir" but "which he can no longer live up to."[6]

Treatments of spiritual bankruptcy in the Age of Hawthorne are especially illuminating because Hawthorne had also provided ample inspiration for the image of the Puritan as solitary seeker a generation before. A quarter-century after Paul Elmer More's "The Solitude of Nathaniel Hawthorne," Lewis Mumford opened his chapter "Twilight" in *The Golden Day: A Study in American Experience and Culture* with the lines: "Hawthorne was the afterglow of the Seventeenth Century. With him came the twilight of Puritanism as a spiritual force. . . . In Hawthorne . . . the conviction which produced a Paradise Lost or a Pilgrim's Progress still glowed with a white intensity; but its heat was gone. Hawthorne was silver; the silver of moonlight; the silver of fine goblets; the tarnished silver of ancient and abandoned houses, locked in moldy drawers."[7] Closer in time to "Solitude," a much more conventional literary historian than Mumford, Hall Frye, used the image of sound rather than of light to depict the world in which liberal Protestantism and secular romanticism supplanted a grim but tough Calvinist theology. The motives and impulses of those, like Hawthorne and many of his characters, who had lost the religion of early New England, were, he wrote, "like faint and incoherent echoes of a long-forgotten tune."[8] At about the same time, Paul More helped mark the centenary of Hawthorne's birthday in 1904 by evoking what was, and would remain, one of the most familiar images of Hawthorne's world and, by transference, of the world of the early twentieth-century young intellectual: "He came just when the moral ideas of New England were passing from the conscience to the imagination and just before the slow, withering process of decay set in"—before, that is, those ideas became simply irritants for the nerves.[9] Although Puritanism still tugged at Hawthorne's conscience and that of his characters, his relationship to it came to symbolize, as it was symbolized in his stories, a pale reflection that only occasionally became

---

[6] Paul Elmer More, "Hawthorne and Poe," *Shelburne Essays* (New York: Phaeton Press, First Series, 1904), 69–70; William MacDonald's review of James Truslow Adams's *The Founding of New England*, in *NAR* 204 (September 1921): 425; Benjamin DeCasseres, "The American," *American Mercury* 10 (February 1927): 146–47.

[7] Lewis Mumford, *The Golden Day: A Study in American Experience and Culture* (New York: Boni & Liveright, 1926), 138.

[8] Hall Frye, *Literary Reviews and Criticisms* (Freeport, N.Y.: Books for Libraries Press, 1908), 124.

[9] Paul Elmer More, "Hawthorne: Looking Before and After," *Shelburne Essays* (Second Series, 1905), 172, 181. On the theme of modern Puritanism as an irritant to the nerves see Alfred B. Kuttner, "Nerves," in *Civilization in the United States*, ed. Harold Stearns (Westport, Conn.: Greenwood Press, 1972 [1922]), 438–41; Harvey O'Higgins, "The Nervous American," *AM* 63 (March 1929): 257–63; Frederick E. Pierce, "Nervous New England," *NAR* 210 (July 1919): 81–85.

more vivid, or something insubstantial for which there was only an occasional grasp. As such, that relationship spoke most persuasively to the more conservative or traditionalist critics of America's spiritual deficiency in the twentieth century, those who hoped that perhaps some residue or memory of Puritanism might again "summon up that greatness of spirit in which Hester, for example, faces life, once her most painful part has been acted out."[10]

The Education of Henry Adams, and the images of a relationship to Puritanism it suggested, appealed more widely than the Age of Hawthorne to young intellectuals seeking a contemporary mode of expressing their spiritual ennui. To the traditionalists, *The Education* recorded the unfortunate slide from idealism into naturalism from which they, unlike the brother of Brooks and Charles Francis Adams, Jr., expected the nation to recover. To the dissidents, on the other hand, *The Education* was like a preface to their own open, willful rejection of what were allegedly Puritan ideals and their embrace of the vitality and love of life that they believed Adams meant by the term *Force*. In the words of Waldo Frank's *Our America*, Adams "died wistfully worshiping the mystery of Force, adoring the blind fecundity of woman: with faint hands groping after Life which of all things the Puritan had no doctrine and no technique to embrace."[11] Thus Adams, unlike Hawthorne, escaped the spiritual bankruptcy of his generation, although both traditionalists and dissidents agreed that the resolution the tensions in Adams's life achieved was genuinely tragic. With an awareness of profound spiritual loss, Robert Herrick noted that Adams's escape "from the too intolerable consciousness of sin" meant that he also no longer had "the invitation or the capacity to sin."[12] T. K. Whipple, from a more dissident perspective, welcomed Adams's acceptance of naturalism, while at the same time admitting that it had entailed the frustrating defeat of Adams's more spiritual self.[13] In both cases, the sense of tragedy indicated the seriousness with which America's young thinkers viewed their own and their nation's spiritual bankruptcy.

Dialectical Analysis and the Transcendence of the Puritan Tradition

The existential tension created by the paradoxical relationship of America's young intellectuals toward Puritanism found expression not only in the treatments of Hawthorne and Adams but also in an especially apt form of historical analysis. The form was dialectical, representing at various levels the experience of spiritual bankruptcy beneath it, just as

[10] Mumford, *Golden Day*, 142.
[11] Frank, *Our America*, 170.
[12] Robert Herrick, "New England and the Novel," *Nation* 111 (September 18, 1920): 325.
[13] T.K. Whipple, "Henry Adams: The First Modern," *Nation* 122 (April 4, 1926): 408–09.

the experiences of the decline of New England, the rise of professional scholarship, and the passing of the Age of Emerson found peculiar expression in the late nineteenth-century critical analyses of Puritanism. Dialectical analysis in the early twentieth century embodied paradox in the thesis of traditional Puritan vitality and the antithesis of waning spirituality. It also absorbed the yearning for spiritual renewal and the pursuit of a new language suited to post-Puritan idealism in the synthesis. The dialectic, in other words, both contained and released the tension created by the experience of Puritan hegemony in its moment of spiritual decline. Dialectical analysis also lent itself to an advance in the historical criticism of Puritanism. Adapting the professional historians' method of highlighting cleavages in America's development, the historical dialectic conceived of Puritan culture as the thesis; an alternative tradition, such as pioneering, was the antithesis challenging the hegemony of Puritan culture; and a new, pluralistic culture, still in embryo, was the synthesis. Examined dialectically, Puritanism no more contained all the possibilities of America's cultural development in the twentieth century than it had of the nation's political development in the late nineteenth. Cultural filio-pietism could be rejected as uncategorically as historical filio-pietism had been.

Van Wyck Brooks's *The Wine of the Puritans* first put forward the dialectical interpretation of America's cultural past in 1908, which George Santayana, one of Brooks's mentors at Harvard, expanded two years later in his highly influential "The Genteel Tradition in American Philosophy." Brooks in turn reworded Santayana's conceptualization in *America's Coming-of-Age.* Together with H. L. Mencken's famous "Puritanism as a Literary Force" and the elaboration of one of Mencken's ideas by Randolph Bourne in "The Puritan's Will to Power," all of which were published in one form or another before the end of World War I, these five pieces contain most of the tools used by the dissident intellectuals to chart the past but now receding power of the Puritan tradition in the 1920s. Employing the dialectical mode of analysis, they not only portrayed Puritanism receding but also dictated the form the final attempt to hold on to Puritanism would have to take. Best articulated by Stuart Sherman and examined in the last chapter, Puritanism's last stand would have to be an attack on historicism, on relativism, on the modern mind's acceptance of transience. It would have to be a reassertion of the eternal, of absolutes, of the universality of the Right.

"You put the old wine into new bottles," Van Wyck Brooks wrote in 1908, "and when the explosion results, one may say, the aroma passes into the air and the wine spills on the floor. The aroma, or the ideal, turns into transcendentalism, and the wine, or the real, becomes commercialism. In any case, one doesn't preserve a great deal of well-tempered, genial wine."[14] The old wine had been a synthesis of old world Puritanism and the new world pressures of pioneering, reinforcing each other in the ethics of industry and thrift. But the Puritan element could not accustom itself to the material prosperity of the nation beginning in the second quarter of the nineteenth century; and the weakening of the New England idea that followed left American culture without cohesion.

The aroma of the old wine had all but disappeared by the beginning of the twentieth century, but the stale odors of asceticism and acquisi- 𝓋 tiveness remained. Puritanism was traditionally held responsible for both, but some of Brooks's followers shifted the blame to the pioneering component of the old wine synthesis, hoping that the recent passing of the frontier would result as well in the passing of disdain for such products of leisure as art and literature and of the other middle-class vices accompanying acquisitiveness. They tried, in other words, to augment the historical significance of the pioneering tradition and diminish that of the Puritan.[15] The purpose of *The Wine of the Puritans* was, after all, to inspire a new generation to build a new tradition, a new synthesis, on the ruins of the New England idea. Brooks admitted that "we fancy that we enjoy our bewilderment, but deep down we are all longing for something definite, something absolute, something solid."[16] While his dialectical perspective on the American past suggested to some the exploration for a usable past in the positive contributions of pioneering to the American spirit, George Santayana found inspiration in Brooks's observation that, in Santayana's words, "America is a young country with an old mentality."[17]

Santayana began "The Genteel Tradition in American Philosophy," as Brooks had begun *The Wine of the Puritans*, with the image of "old wine in new bottles"; although for Santayana, of Spanish descent, the old wine was not just old world Puritanism but the entire English race and

---

[14] Van Wyck Brooks, "The Wine of the Puritans," in *Van Wyck Brooks: The Early Years*, 6.

[15] The relationship between Puritanism and pioneering soon became a popular subject among cultural commentators. Brooks expanded his analysis in "The Culture of Industrialism," *Seven Arts* 1 (April 1917): 655–66. Also see Waldo Frank, *The Re-discovery of America* (New York: Scribner's, 1929), 106, 185; and *Our America*, 63 passim; Horace Kallen, *Culture and Democracy in the United States* (New York: Boni & Liveright, 1970 [1924]), 217; Mumford, *Golden Day*, 73–74; John Macy, "A Glance at the Real Puritans," *Harper's* 154 (May 1927): 748–50; Harvey O'Higgins and Edward Reede, *The American Mind in Action* (New York: Harper & Bros., 1920), 11; Harold Stearns, *America and the Young Intellectual* (New York: George H. Doran, 1921), 35; and William Carlos Williams, *In the American Grain* (New York: New Directions, 1956 [1925]), chapters "The Maypole of Merry Mount" and "Pere Sebastian Rasles."

[16] Brooks, "The Wine of the Puritans," 58–59.

[17] Santayana, "The Genteel Tradition in American Philosophy," 39. The passage in Brooks's "The Wine of the Puritans" is from pages 8–12.

culture. His dialectic of American cultural development then took the form of an antithesis between the old mentality of the fathers, dominating "the higher things of the mind" and eventually declining into the genteel tradition, and the new mentality, "an expression of the instincts, practice, and discoveries of the younger generations," taking the form of "aggressive enterprise." The point at which the two mentalities decisively separated from their common Calvinist origin was for Santayana, as for Brooks, when the appearance of Transcendentalism heralded the rise of prosperity and optimism in the mid-nineteenth century.[18]

Surpassing Brooks's mere hope for a new cultural synthesis, Santayana claimed that William James had already made such a synthesis possible by the bold discovery, and subsequent exposure, of the genteel tradition itself. James, according to Santayana, "has overcome the genteel tradition in the classic way, by understanding it." James's evolutionary method challenged the genteel confidence in a created universe, and his pragmatic standard of judgment concluded that the genteel tradition had lost its capacity "to prepare us to meet events, as future experience may unroll them." Because James had taken this first step, it was only a matter of time before the entire old mentality in which the genteel tradition was rooted, English Calvinism, would also be overcome: "When the child is too vigorous for that, he will develop a fresh mentality of his own, out of his own observations and actual instincts; and this fresh mentality will interfere with the traditional mentality, and tend to reduce it to something perfunctory, conventional, and perhaps secretly despised."[19]

In *America's Coming-of-Age*, Van Wyck Brooks suggested that this fresh mentality would occupy a "middle ground" between the "highbrow" mentality of stark theory, dessicated culture, piety, and the feminine; and the "lowbrow" mentality of stark business, utility, advertisement, and the masculine. Heretofore such a middle ground had been impossible in the United States because

> without doubt the Puritan Theocracy is the all-influential fact in the history of the American mind. It was the Puritan conception of the Deity as not alone all-determining but precisely responsible for the practical affairs of the race, as constituting in fact, the State itself, which precluded in advance any central bond, any responsibility, any common feeling in American affairs and which justified the unlimited centrifugal expediency which has always marked American life. And the same instinct that made against centrality in government made against centrality in thought, against common standards of any kind. The imminent eternal issue the Puritans felt so keenly, and the equally imminent practical issues they experienced so monotonously threw

---

[18] Santayana, "The Genteel Tradition," 39–40, 42.
[19] *Ibid.*, 54–59, 39.

almost no light on one another; there was no middle ground between to mitigate, combine, or harmonize them.

Yet Brooks's generation knew that middle ground "as an appetite" for a common culture based on the uninhibited experience of the common life of the American people. Although in 1915 Brooks was still unclear about the details of what a synthesis of the highbrow and lowbrow mentalities would be like, he evidently believed it would herald the end of the dialectical development of the American mind, for in the final analysis common culture occupies "the genial middle ground of human tradition."[20]

To H. L. Mencken, America's early twentieth-century culture was already all too common. Contrary to Brooks, Mencken believed the culture was already based on a tradition, an inhuman one; and although that tradition was itself in decline, its influence, regrettably, was not. The interaction of the internal development of Puritan philosophy, on one hand, and the pressure of changing socioeconomic conditions, on the other, told for Mencken in "Puritanism as a Literary Force" the whole story of American culture. In the early stages of American history, Puritanism was a stern but, Mencken admitted, noble philosophy, uniting the "conviction of the pervasiveness of sin" and "of the supreme importance of moral correctness" with a genuine interest in "the mysteries" and a fear of "missing their correct solution." Between the Revolution and the Civil War, under the pressure of almost universal poverty—an assertion that Brooks, Santayana, and present day historians would dispute—the original Puritan was transformed into the "ameliorated Puritan." Poverty softened the hard lines of the older Puritans, making them too humble and too poor to carry their war against sin outside their own souls and to the conduct of their neighbors, a practice not unknown to the first colonists but not habitual with them either. After the Civil War, however, prosperity in general and the accumulation of wealth by certain individuals in particular brought the "wholesale transvaluation of Values," as Nietzsche's American disciple called it. The resulting new or Neo-Puritanism was distinguished by "the transfer of ire from the Old Adam to the happy rascal across the street" and "the sinister rise of a New Inquisition in the midst of a growing luxury." Again borrowing from Nietzsche, Mencken labeled the new motive behind Neo-Puritanism the *Wille zur Macht* or will to power, first detecting it in the passage of the "Comstock Postal Act" of 1873 and the subsequent formation of Anthony Comstock's New York Society for the Suppression of Vice.[21] Whether

---

[20] Van Wyck Brooks, "America's Coming-of-Age," in *Van Wyck Brooks: The Early Years*, 83–84, 86, 92, 111, 120.

[21] H. L. Mencken, "Puritanism as a Literary Force," in Mencken, *A Book of Prefaces* (Garden City, N.Y.: Garden City Publishing Co., 1927 [1917]), 226–27, 232–35. On Anthony Comstock see his "official" biography by Charles Gallaudet Trumbull, *Anthony*

Mencken ever saw a significant challenge to Neo-Puritanism in the changing socioeconomic conditions of his own time, or a real hope for a new cultural synthesis, is unclear.

By making Neo-Puritanism, and especially the vice crusade, the focus of his cultural commentary, Mencken came under attack for being a crusader himself. Randolph Bourne, who shared Mencken's disdain for common culture and who was indebted to Mencken for the conception of the will-to-power motive behind Neo-Puritanism, nevertheless asked in reviewing Mencken's A Book of Prefaces in 1917, "How is it that so robust a hater of uplift and puritanism becomes so fanatical a crusader himself?" noting that, especially in "Puritanism as a Literary Force," Mencken was "the moralist contra moralism, run . . . amuck."[22] This trait of Mencken's was, at the very least, inconvenient for Bourne, who saw his own role in the critique of Puritanism as destroyer of the credibility of the crusader. Contrary to "popular superstition," Bourne asserted, the crusader did not have "an extra endowment of moral force" but was, rather, "just as much of a naturalistic phenomenon as the most carnal sinner." The concept of the will to power called attention to the way in which the Puritan "cunningly organized [the] satisfaction of two of his strongest impulses,—the self-conscious personal impulses of being re-garded and being neglected." The first step of the "puritan process" was the satisfaction of the impulse for neglect in the form of genuine self-abasement or renunciation. Even the Puritan, however, recognized this self-control as "the dreariest of all satisfactions of the will to power" and, therefore, took the second step to fulfill the impulse to be regarded by becoming proud of his self-control: "the renouncing must be made into an ideal, the ideal must be codified, promulgated, and in the last analysis, enforced."[23]

Having analyzed the motive behind Neo-Puritanism in these terms, Bourne then went one step further and in so doing distinguished himself from other dissident critics of the influence of Puritanism on American cultural development. Bourne believed that most people were unable to take pride in renunciation and so became pagan, the very opposite of being Puritan. Paganism and Puritanism did not, however, offer hope

---

Comstock, Fighter (New York: Fleming H. Revell, 1913) and the more balanced work by Heywood Broun and Mary Leach, Anthony Comstock, Roundsman of the Lord (New York: Literary Guild of America, 1927).

[22] Randolph Bourne's review of Mencken's A Book of Prefaces, NR 13 (November 24, 1917): 102.

[23] Randolph Bourne, "The Puritan's Will to Power," History of a Literary Radical and Other Essays (New York: Biblio & Tanner, 1969[1920]), 179–87. Discussions of the Puritan's will to power other than Mencken's and Bourne's include Mumford, Golden Day, 87; Bertrand Russell, "The Revival of Puritanism," Freeman 8 (October 17, 1923): 130; Harold Stearns, Liberalism in America (New York: Boni & Liveright, 1919), 53, 63; and Arthur Train, Puritan's Progress (New York: Scribner's, 1931), 452–54.

for a cultural synthesis, according to Bourne, but rather perpetually coexisted in the American character. Thus, it was pointless to regret the persistence of Puritanism or, for that matter, to become confident in one's paganism: "if there were no puritans we should have to invent them" because "no one can be really a good appreciating pagan who has not once been a bad puritan."[24]

Idealism Beyond Puritanism?

From Van Wyck Brooks's call for a culture emanating from the common life of the American people, to Randolph Bourne's assertion that paganism and Puritanism coexist in the American character, the nation's leading dissident intellectuals sought an organic relationship between national values and the national past. This relationship was precisely what had been lost when New England's Protestant establishment divided into the genteel moralizers and the radical demythologizers after the Civil War. Twice before New England's leaders had disagreed about the proper adaptation of the Puritan tradition, when the Calvinists and Unitarians battled for hegemony in the first four decades of the nineteenth century and when moderate reformers tried to restrain the higher law moralists in the 1850s. On neither of these two occasions was the Puritan past used to subvert the claims of either side—indeed it strengthened all sides; hence, the link between history and culture was preserved and the Puritan tradition remained alive. But when the link was severed in the late nineteenth century, Puritanism rather than its interpreters was blamed. Indicative of the higher regard for secular scholarship than for theological and moral reinterpretation, critics believed the historians' and blamed the genteel idealists' renderings of the Puritan impulse. If the Puritan temperament isolated the Emersonian generation from the common life of its period, then something in the Puritan spirit also made for the more profound isolation of ideals from reality in American culture as a whole. The task of Brooks's and Bourne's generation was to offer new interpretations of reality, including the American past, in the hope of cultivating fertile ground for its ideals. Seeking a return to what its most articulate members believed was Puritanism's original organic impulse, binding ideals to reality, the Lost Generation nevertheless also showed that the Puritan legacy it had inherited was no longer a usable past.

[24] Bourne, "The Puritan's Will to Power," 176.

10

The Unusable Past

In 1918, the Committee on Public Information published a pamphlet by Stuart Sherman, an English professor at the University of Illinois, entitled "American and Allied Ideals, an Appeal to Those Who are Neither Hot nor Cold." Rejecting the contention that Puritanism itself had devolved into the isolation of ideals from reality, Sherman placed the responsibility for this acknowledged development squarely on the shoulders of Puritanism's intellectual critics. Together with H. L. Mencken's popularization of the critique of Puritanism in *American Mercury* during the 1920s, Sherman's pamphlet further enflamed a controversy that prewar dissidents had hoped to place in cold storage. As early as the 1920 tricentennial celebration of the landing of the Pilgrims, the historian Charles Beard tried to call a truce between the "ego-maniacs," led by Sherman, who were sympathetic toward the genteel tradition, and the "improvers of America," led by Mencken, who "will burst upon our affrighted gaze in full war paint, knife in teeth, a tomahawk dripping with ink in one hand, a stein of Pilsner in the other." To the egomaniacs, Puritanism stood for "Godliness, Thrift, Liberty, Democracy, Culture, Industry, Frugality, Temperance, Resistance to tyranny, Pluck, Principle, A free church, A free state, Equal rights, A holy Sabbath, Liberty under law, Individual freedom, Self-government, The gracious spirit of Christianity." To the improvers of America, however, Puritanism stood for "Philistinism, Harsh restraint, Beauty-hating, Stout-faced fanaticism, Supreme hypocrisy, Canting, Demonology, Enmity to true art, Intellectual tyranny, Grape juice, Grisly sermons, Religious persecution, Sullenness, Ill-temper, Stinginess, Bigotry, Conceit, Bombast." But Beard's humor and call for restraint were out of step with the times. Before the decade was over, and not without a debate of greater intellectual integrity than Beard might have imagined, the improvers of America could claim victory.[1]

Stuart Sherman and the Regeneration of the Puritan Tradition

Stuart Sherman was a member of the same generation as Mencken. When World War I broke out, both believed that the conflict might

---

[1] Charles A. Beard, "On Puritans," *New Republic* 25 (December 1, 1920): 15-17.

√ become the instrument of America's spiritual regeneration.[2] Sherman, however, was an intellectual who hoped that the nation would rise up to meet Puritan standards, especially Puritanism's traditional sacrificial virtues, rather than, like Mencken, one who hoped America would rise up against Puritan standards. In "American and Allied Ideals" Sherman voiced his aspiration in terms of four propositions about contemporary America, two of which indicated the obstacles to be overcome before spiritual regeneration could occur, and two of which explained why the regeneration of Puritanism was America's best hope for spiritual renewal. These propositions later became the scaffolding on which the crescendo of debate about American Puritanism rose in the decade following the war, finally collapsing into indifference by 1930.

The obstacles in the way of America's spiritual regeneration were, according to Sherman, two groups subversive of America's national purpose. One group consisted of immigrants who "have come to America and applied for the privileges of citizenship without any intention of becoming citizens in spirit," who "preserve unmixed in this country the culture of the country from which they came, and wherever possible . . . perpetuate their mother tongue as the preferred language." The other group was composed of men of literature and professors who "sneer at the ideals and professions of democratic government . . . at the Pilgrim Fathers and at all the Puritans who since the seventeenth century have constituted the moral backbone of the nation" and who "celebrate . . . the literature of Berlin and Vienna, especially the nastiest part of it which they are certain will offend what they scoffingly call the Puritanical sensibilities of Americans."[3]

Critics of Puritanism were almost as offended by the ethnocentrism of Sherman's pamphlet as they were by its criticism of cosmopolitan intellectuals because the pluralism of modern American society was the reality that had inspired their call for a new mentality in the United States in the first place. Mencken exposed the nativism behind "American and Allied Ideals" by reporting Sherman to have said that "Puritanism is the official philosophy of America, and that all who dispute it are enemy aliens and should be deported." Ernest Boyd reviewed the publication of Sherman's *On Contemporary Literature* in a *Nation* article entitled "Ku Klux Kriticism," claiming that Sherman wanted "to rehabilitate Puritanism" by making all "American literature . . . Nordic, Protestant, and

---

[2] On the relationship between Puritanism and World War I see especially the following *New Republic* articles: Francis Hackett, "Lilies of the Field" and William Allen White's letter to the editor, 19 (May 17, 1919): 84–85, 88; and F. B. Kay, "Puritanism, Literature, and War," 25 (December 15, 1920): 64–67.

[3] Stuart Sherman, "American and Allied Ideals, An Appeal to Those Who are Neither Hot nor Cold" (Washington, D.C.: Committee on Public Information, February, 1918), *War Information Series*, No. 12, 6–9.

blond."[4] Although Sherman's postwar defense of Puritanism avoided the blatant ethnocentrism of his earlier statements, that of his followers sometimes did not. After Sherman's death in 1926, Paul Elmer More, along with Irving Babbitt, carried on Puritanism's defense, and More's *A New England Group and Others*, for example, blamed "the clamour of our emancipated youth, hailing largely from stranger lands in the dark map of Europe" for tempting Americans "to miss the more fragile beauty of New England," which "is the fairest thing this country has produced."[5] Although such principles of cultural criticism represented what most repelled the Menckens about America, the nativism of "neo-Puritanism" in the 1920s remained something of a peripheral issue.

Sherman's implication in "American and Allied Ideals" that anti-Puritan intellectuals were largely ignorant of America's genuinely Puritan sensibilities also became a peripheral issue in the twenties, but for a different reason. Critics of Puritanism quickly realized that the struggle to keep the development of American culture on its appointed dialectical course required them to know the enemy inside and out. A *New Republic* reviewer of Elizabeth Deering Hascom's *The Heart of the Puritan: Selections from Letters and Journals* admitted in 1918 that "so long as our ideas about Puritanism are derived from the memories of the manners and morals of the small towns of the Middle West since the Civil War, of the-things-that-mustn't-be-talked-about, so long as we fail to grasp any of the spring of thought and action of the genuine Puritan, we are not going to criticize him intelligently." Reflecting the disappointment of many of the young that the Puritan hegemony could not be broken, the reviewer mused:

> Will some good conservative kindly buy up the edition [of *The Heart of the Puritan*] for free distribution among our serious young writers under thirty-five who never read anything American earlier than Henry James? . . . For, above all, the book shows that our forefathers had an intenseness about things which makes our intenseness seem half-hearted and indecisive. Which is probably the reason why our young moderns have not, as yet, ridden the Puritan spirit out of town on its appointed rail. It is far too alive and kicking.[6]

---

[4] On Sherman's nativism see H. L. Mencken, "Variations on a Familiar Theme," *Smart Set* 66 (December 1921): 139; and two selections from *Criticism in America: Its Function and Status* (New York: Harcourt, Brace, 1924): H. L. Mencken, "Criticism of Criticism of Criticism," 179, and Ernest Boyd, "Ku Klux Kriticism," 309–20.

[5] Paul Elmer More, *A New England Group and Others*, in *Shelburne Essays* (Eleventh Series, 1921), 31.

[6] Review of Elizabeth Deering Hascom's *The Heart of the Puritans*, in *NR* 16 (August 17, 1918): 85. Other discussions of the timeliness of this publication include the letter headed "Liberal New England and Western Prudery," *NR* 16 (September 7, 1918): 171, and the rejoinder "Puritanic Taboos," *NR* 16 (September 28, 1918): 260 and H. L. Mencken, "Literae Humaniores," *SS* 14 (March 1918): 138.

The defenders and opponents of Puritanism never agreed what the "spring of thought and action of the genuine Puritan" was, but not much print was wasted during the twenties accusing each other of ignorance. The conflict had early come to focus on Stuart Sherman's two assertions about why Puritanism was America's best spiritual and cultural hope.

Since the purpose of "American and Allied Ideals" was to convince the sceptical that the United States was fighting for something very important in World War I, Sherman first denied Van Wyck Brooks's contention that the nation lacked a culture. Not only, Sherman claimed, did America have a culture based on Puritan morality, public education, and democracy; but it was also extremely vital. To look beyond Puritanism for America's spiritual renewal was, therefore, unnecessary. It was also unwise. In the international conflict against Germany, Puritanism—presumably only Puritanism—could resist the spread of the German ideal of "inner freedom and external control." The American ideal was "external freedom and inner control," based on the Puritan "inner check upon the expansion of natural impulse"; and in a society living according to this ideal "the individual looks after his conduct and the Government looks after his liberty." In other words, America's culture was essentially a civic rather than an artistic culture, founded on the principle of civil liberty and made possible by the Puritan habit of internalizing the restraints on individual passion necessary to civil order.[7]

Sherman's definition of Puritanism as the "inner check upon the expansion of natural instinct" had an immense impact on America's interpretation of the Puritan tradition in the 1920s. Intellectual critics of Puritanism were initially overjoyed to have from the pen of one so sympathetic to the Puritan tradition a characterization so damning. The twenties was, after all, the decade in which Sigmund Freud's diagnosis of the consequences of psychological repression achieved its greatest popularity. Harvey O'Higgins and Edward H. Reede's 1920 psychoanalytic expose of America's Puritan writers entitled *The American Mind in Action* made a case against the artistic oppressiveness of Puritanism on almost the same grounds as Sherman had made the case for the civic value of Puritan restraint.[8] Careful readers of Sherman, however, understood not only that artistic oppressiveness and civic restraint were not interchangeable but also that Sherman was trying to make the health of America's political culture, rather than its literary culture, the true test of the vitality of Puritanism in the twentieth century. The confidence with which Sherman and his followers affirmed the Puritan contribution to America's political culture at first understandably worried Puritanism's prewar critics. But as the

---

[7] Sherman, "American and Allied Ideals," 6–9.

[8] Hoffman, *The Twenties;* Robert Crunden, *From Self to Society, 1919–1941* (Englewood Cliffs, N.J.: Prentice–Hall, 1972); O'Higgins and Reede, *American Mind in Action.*

degeneration of American politics during the twenties into what William Leuchtenburg has so aptly called "political fundamentalism" accelerated, they began to realize that the cultural hegemony of Puritanism would finally be broken before the decade ended.[9]

Puritanism as America's Defense against Modernism

The defenders of America's Puritan tradition in the 1920s at first either ignored or refused to accept the prewar reassessment of Puritanism, simply offering a positive version of the literary and cultural developments already condemned by Puritanism's critics as filio-pietism. Carl Van Doren in *The American Novel*, for example, traced to the present the "tradition of conscience" in the United States on which Puritan New England had made its distinctive imprint. In *Culture and Democracy in the United States*, Horace Kallen not only called attention to the consciousness of conscience in New England but also noted that "for New England, religious, political and literary interests remained coordinate and undivided" during much of the nineteenth century, concluding that "New England gave the tone to and established the standards for the rest of American society." In *Democratic Distinction in America*, W. C. Brownell traced the way in which the Puritan tradition in ethics achieved "national stature" by the second decade of the nineteenth century and still remained the basis for the national earnestness and seriousness of purpose.[10] The only potential threat to the prewar analysis of Puritanism in these studies was their rejection of the dialectical method with which Puritanism's critics had exposed the fragmentation of the Puritan tradition and prophesied the emergence of a new American culture.

A new but seemingly minor twist did appear with the association of Walt Whitman and the Puritan tradition. No one in American letters was more superficially antagonistic to Puritanism, nor more of a beacon of liberation to young dissidents, than Walt Whitman. Yet after World War I, the literary critics Emerson Grant Sutcliffe and Percy Boynton both placed Whitman inside rather than in opposition to the New England literary tradition. Sutcliffe called attention to Whitman's indebtedness to Emerson, while Boynton portrayed Whitman as a moral critic of European decadence. By 1929, even the radical Waldo Frank located Whitman along with Emerson and Thoreau in "the mystic tradition"

---

[9] William Leuchtenburg, *The Perils of Prosperity* (Chicago: Univ. of Chicago Press, 1958).

[10] Carl Van Doren, *The American Novel* (New York: Macmillan, 1921). Robert Morss Lovett called Van Doren's theme the "tradition of conscience" in his *New Republic* review, 29 (December 21, 1921), 107; Kallen, *Culture and Democracy*, 81, 215; W. C. Brownell, *Democratic Distinction in America* (New York: Scribner's, 1927), 137–39.

that the Puritans made "organic."[11]

The inclusion of the egalitarian Whitman is too obvious a case in point, but the strategy of the defenders of Puritanism gradually emerging was to argue that any intellectual who stood outside the Puritan tradition was not a fit contributor to democratic culture. This begins to become clear in the conservative attack on modernism. Modernism is at least as difficult to define as any other "ism," and probably more so. To the followers of Stuart Sherman it meant the obsession with "inner freedom" that led in Europe to "external control." Accordingly, in *A New England Group*, Paul Elmer More called upon the Puritan spirit to save twentieth-century America from the irresponsibility of modernist intellectuals, just as the Puritan mind had "impregnably fortified" American romanticism from the dissolution of character typical of romantic intellectuals on the Continent in the nineteenth century. Not Neo-Puritan prudery, but the ancestral Puritan fear of God was the key to the modern salvation of America, for as Harvey Wickham later observed in *The Impuritans*, modernism is "the abandonment of Christian faith coupled with an unwillingness to take the logical consequences," including the inability to account for either the physical world or human consciousness.[12] Even George Santayana, once the senior critic of Puritan influence on American cultural development, came to see that the Puritan tradition was America's best hope for escaping modernism. Commenting on the widely-discussed symposium, *Civilization in the United States*, he observed that "Americanism, apart from the genteel tradition, is simply modernism." Having once inspired H. L. Mencken and George Nathan to conclude that "Puritanism and Americanism are really no more than two names for the same thing," Santayana now warned dissident intellectuals that their efforts to create a new American culture exclusive of the Puritan tradition threatened to subordinate American experience to the decadence of European cultural development.[13]

---

[11] For the traditional view of Walt Whitman see Brooks, "America's Coming-of-Age," 128–30, 135–36, and Santayana, "The Genteel Tradition in American Philosophy," 52–53; Emerson Grant Sutcliffe, "Whitman, Emerson, and the New Poetry," *NR* 19 (May 24, 1919): 114–15; Percy Boynton, "American Literature and the Tart Set," *Freeman* (April 7, 1920): 88–89; Frank, *Rediscovery of America*, 214–18.

[12] More, *A New England Group*, 83; Harvey Wickham, *The Impuritans* (Freeport, N.Y.: Books for Libraries Press, 1970 [1929]), 90 passim. Dorothy Brewster believed that More was pointing toward an ancestral fear of God in her review of *A New England Group*, in *Nation* 113 (July 27, 1921): 101; and Stuart Sherman called More's goal a "revived sense of sin" in *The Emotional Discovery of America and Other Essays* (Freeport, N.Y.: Books for Libraries Press, 1932), 49.

[13] George Santayana, "Marginal Notes on *Civilization in the United States*," in *The Genteel Tradition*, 135; H. L. Mencken and George Nathan, "Repetition Generale," *SS* 64 (April 1921): 42. Jackson Lear's *No Place For Grace: Anti-modernism and the Transformation of American Culture* (New York: Pantheon Books, 1981) is a provocative recent

Not surprisingly, it was Stuart Sherman who made the strategy of
attacking modernism explicit. It is also interesting that he began, in his
Pilgrim tricentennial article in *Atlantic* entitled "What is a Puritan?"
with a feint in the direction of his critics' intense concern with the
responsibility of American intellectuals for America's spiritual health.
"We are not exceptionally rich in spiritual traditions," Sherman acknowledged. And, he continued,

> it would be a pity, by a persistent campaign of abuse to ruin the
> credit of any good ones. One of the primary functions, indeed, of
> scholarship and letters is to connect us with the great traditions and
> to inspire us with the confidence and power which result from such a
> connection. Puritanism, rightly understood, is one of the vital, pro-
> gressive, and enriching human traditions. It is a tradition peculiarly
> necessary to the health and stability and the safe forward movement
> of a democratic society. When I consider from what antiquity it has
> come down to us and what vicissitudes it has survived, I do not fear
> its extermination; but I resent the misapprehension of its character
> and the aspersion of its name.

The misapprehension of Puritanism resulted, according to Sherman,
from the mistaken identification of the will to power as the dominant
motive behind the development of the Puritan tradition. In reality that
motive was the will to perfection, successively embodied in the affirmation of individual reason, the promotion of enlightenment, and the "disdain for formalism and routine which made Puritanism profoundly in
sympathy with the modern spirit" because of its "disposition to accept
nothing on authority, but to bring all reports to the test of experience."[14]

The will to perfection differentiated the modern spirit of Puritanism
from the spirit of modernism by giving the test of experience a moral
standard rather than elevating experimentalism into an end in itself. The
modernist who did elevate experimentalism into an end in itself lacked
the ability to direct the growth of democracy because he failed to unite
his freedom of intelligence with stability of character. The Puritan, on
the other hand, effected this necessary union: "Because his radical intellect is steadily in the service of his passion for perfection, his character
can be trusted for stability and amendment, as, from age to age, men
improve the quality of the positive customs and beliefs which they place
under the protection of God."[15]

If the modernist critics of Puritanism wanted American culture to
become more vital and instinctual, Sherman insisted, they had to realize
that the will to perfection was itself an instinct. They lacked this realization because the instinct for perfection was grounded in the reality of a

---

book on this subject.

[14] Stuart Sherman, "What is a Puritan?" *Atlantic* 128 (September 1921): 345–48.

[15] Sherman, *Emotional Discovery of America*, 56–57.

moral world, and the modernists—not the genteel idealists—did not have the conviction of this reality:

> The moment the monoptic naturalists begin to discuss the moral world, they take [the] line . . . that the moral world is so unreal as to be virtually non-existent—at the same time howling at the thorns which it thrusts into them. The assumption of practically all the insurgents against customs, convention, and morality is that every man who takes a customary, conventional, or moral attitude is a coward and essentially a moral phantom.[16]

How could one hope to discover the common culture of which Van Wyck Brooks dreamed without accepting that the average American "believes it possible to distinguish between good and evil, and . . . also believes that, having made the distinction, [his] welfare depends upon . . . furthering the one and curbing the other"?[17] The development of a common culture required, according to Sherman, that educated persons adopt the "religion of democracy," but to do this, they must first accept the religiosity of demos. They must, in other words, submit themselves to the hegemony of America's Puritan tradition.[18]

By couching his defense of the Puritan tradition in an attack on modernism, Sherman elevated the debate of the twenties far above the reductionism of either Freudian psychology or Mencken's indictment of the Philistine bourgeoisie. Puritanism in the 1920s did not just stand for middle-class hang-ups or middle-class ideology. It stood, at least among its most sophisticated supporters, for a world view that rejected the fragmentation of human experience represented by the modernists' dialectical method as well as the subjectivism of the modernists' desire for "inner freedom." American culture was of a whole cloth, according to Puritanism's defenders, spun from the belief in a universal moral order, the human instinct for perfection embodying that order in the individual, a respect for religion giving expression to that instinct, and a commitment to democracy acknowledging the people's common religious experience. If American intellectuals found this Puritan culture spiritually deficient, the problem was their own alienation from America, not the fault of the culture. "If the great artist, in expressing himself expresses also the society of which he is a part, it should follow . . . that a great American artist must express the 'profound moral idealism' of America."[19] He might express this

---

16 Stuart Sherman, "On Falling in Love," *Points of View* (New York: Scribner's, 1924), 140.

17 Stuart Sherman, "The National Genius," *Criticism in America*, 240.

18 Sherman, in "The National Genius," 252, and Irving Babbitt, in *Leadership and Democracy* (Boston: Houghton Mifflin, 1924), 254–55, singled out Theodore Dreiser, and especially his important essay "Life, Art and America," *SA* 1 (February 1917): 363–89, as representative of the modernists' disdain for the religiosity of the American public.

19 Sherman, "The National Genius," 252.

idealism differently from other citizens; indeed, one of the most constructive tasks he could perform, Sherman believed, was showing the people how to satisfy their instinct for perfection by the higher "things of the mind and the imagination."[20] But to pretend that Puritanism was something other than moral idealism or that some principle other than moral idealism was the formative principle of American culture was to admit a moral isolation more antisocial than that of any Puritan artist.

The Fatal Link Between Puritanism and Mass Democracy

Alienation and moral isolation are such accurate descriptions of the position of many American intellectuals in the 1920s, it is a wonder that those with New England roots did not finally "return home" to Puritanism as the Southern Agrarians did to their ancestral traditions in the early 1930s. Even those with a healthy respect for moral idealism, however, dissociated themselves from Puritanism by 1930, cultivating in the movement known as the New Humanism Sherman's suggestion that Puritan idealism "is of a sort that the New Englanders shared with Plato and Aristotle."[21] The defection of Irving Babbitt from the defense of Puritanism to the promotion of the New Humanism will serve to demonstrate why Sherman's definition of Puritanism as a comprehensive world view supporting a distinctive civic culture, despite its subtlety and perceptiveness, could not save the Puritan tradition from obsolescence in the 1920s.

In *Democracy and Leadership*, published in 1924, Irving Babbitt used Sherman's "American and Allied Ideals," especially its distinction between Germany's ideal of "inner freedom and external control" and Puritan America's ideal of "inner control and external freedom," as the basis for demanding a revival of genuine democracy in the United States. Like Sherman, Babbitt condemned the disregard for inner control among America's self-proclaimed intellectual leaders; but in contrast to Sherman, who increasingly seemed to identify inner control with private morals and aesthetic preferences, Babbitt continued to identify inner control with political self-restraint. Specifically, Babbitt opposed prohibition and other uses of state power to legislate morality because he feared America's becoming a nation with neither external control nor inner freedom. Genuine democracy, Babbitt acknowledged, was founded on self-control, but the civic culture America had had since prohibition was not genuine democracy. Puritanism, as its most outspoken representatives in the 1920s understood it, was not working. Babbitt and another leader of the New Humanism, W. C. Brownell, whose book *Democratic*

---

[20] Sherman, "The Point of View in American Criticism," in *The Genius of America* (Port Washington, N.Y.: Kennikat Press, 1923), 229–230.
[21] Sherman, "The National Genius," 255. On the New Humanism see Norman Foerster, ed., *Humanism and America* (New York: Farrar & Rinehart, 1930).

Distinction in America appeared in 1927, thus called for a new generation of self-controlled political leaders who could make genuine democracy work by practicing the genuine Puritanism of legislative restraint.[22]

During the Civil War and again during the height of late
nineteenth-century materialism, devotees of the Puritan tradition had also
called for elite leadership modeled on self-abnegation and adherence to the
principle of restraint. But by the third decade of the twentieth century,
total war, the prosperity of the twenties, and the association of Puritanism
with democratic culture made Babbitt's and Brownell's call anachronistic
and ultimately fatal. The manipulation of public opinion by wartime propaganda and the rise of consumer advertising may seem today to have
inaugurated a new kind of elite leadership in the United States; but in the
1920s most observers were more impressed by the newly enlarged role the
masses played in determining the quality of America's self-defense and its
economic health than by the emergence of new elites. Critics of Puritanism
like H. L. Mencken, as well as defenders like Stuart Sherman, realized that
mass democracy was the commanding social reality of the 1920s. They
even agreed that Puritanism and democracy united to form America's distinctive culture. Mencken simply preferred cosmopolitan tolerance to puritanical democracy, whereas Sherman was quite comfortable with the
people's moral idealism.[23] The point is this: during and after World War I,
the Puritan tradition came increasingly to be accepted as the inheritance of
the masses rather than of the elite, and in order for Puritanism to remain
the foundation for a vital national culture it now had to be a civic culture of
the masses, not a literary culture of the elite. Thus when Babbitt and
Brownell admitted that the masses were distorting Puritanism, were per-
verting the Puritan impulse from inner control and external freedom to
external control, they delivered a blow more damaging to the Puritan tradition than any shots delivered by Mencken.

Babbitt and Brownell were hardly alone in confronting the potentially
self-destructive union of Puritanism and democracy in the twentieth century. Prewar intellectuals had after all initially cast twentieth-century
thinking about the Puritan tradition in terms of Puritanism's relationship
to a struggling pluralistic, democratic culture; and during World War I,
Stuart Sherman had obligingly offered American culture the first genuinely nonelitest defense of Puritanism, associating it, finally, with the religion of democracy. Trying to clear Puritanism of responsibility for the
fundamentalist politics of the twenties, some mid-twenties writers further
attested to the problem by trying to reestablish the Puritan tradition as
elitest, suggesting that it had failed to survive the rise of twentieth-century

---

[22] Babbitt, *Leadership and Democracy*, 251–53, and W. C. Brownell, *Democratic Distinction in America*, 50–51.

[23] H. L. Mencken, *Notes on Democracy* (New York: Knopf, 1926), 155–58.

mass democracy. Gilbert Seldes, for example, argued in the *New Republic* that the emotional, democratic spirit of nineteenth-century pietism was the true cause of bigotry in the twenties, not the rational elitest spirit of Puritanism that pietism had replaced. And the Marxist literary critic V. F. Calverton tried to debunk the twenties' "Puritan Myth" in *Scribner's* by showing how the bourgeois spirit of Victorianism supplanted aristocratic Puritanism in the late nineteenth century.[24] But by linking the Puritan tradition so closely with the civic culture of twentieth-century mass democracy, Sherman, Babbitt, and Brownell, like Mencken, facilitated the translation of mounting fears about mass democracy into fears about Puritanism.

Heretofore in the development of the Puritan tradition, Puritanism had assuaged national fears by a vision of redemption, although only the few might claim to see that vision clearly, as when the abolitionists sought to translate the higher law into statutory law. After the twentieth-century democratization of Puritanism, however, national salvation would have had to come from sources broader, not narrower, than the civic culture of Puritanism if that civic culture lacked political restraint. "Our Puritan virtues have lifted us to power and privilege," the Protestant theologian Reinhold Niebuhr wrote in the *Atlantic* in 1926, "but they lack the social imagination to guide us in the use of our power, and they are wanting in the cultural assets to prompt us to a right use of our privileges." "Our Babbitry," Niebuhr continued, referring to Mencken's designation for the conventional and self-righteous mentality of the white Anglo-Saxon Protestant middle class, "is in reality Puritanism gone to seed—a fact which is not lost on the critics of our contemporary civilization who instinctively recognize some affinity between our religious traditions and the moral and cultural limitations of our national life." What America needed, Niebuhr concluded, was "a religion and an ethic which know how to deal with greed as well as with dishonesty, and which have effectual restraints upon the paganism of power and pride as well as upon the paganism of licentious pleasure." Lacking confidence that the Puritan tradition still had the resources to provide such a religion and ethic, Neoorthodoxy's pursuit of justice made no attempt to offer itself as "The New Puritanism."[25] Similarly Babbitt's and Brownell's New Humanism distanced itself from the genteel tradition by finding confirmation of the absolute and eternal truths that might give democracy stability and direction in the oldest traditions of Western civilization rather than in Puritanism. Finally, and most significantly, the initiators of the search for a more usable past found it in secular liberalism, engraved on the

---

[24] Gilbert Seldes, "The Background of Bigotry," *NR* 55 (July 11, 1928): 200; V. F. Calverton, "The Puritan Myth," *Scribner's* 89 (March 1931): 251–57.

[25] Reinhold Niebuhr, "Puritanism and Prosperity," *Atlantic* 137 (June 1926): 725–35.

national consciousness since Richard Hildreth's opposition to George Bancroft's *History*, and especially since the Adams brothers made emancipation from Puritanism the central theme of New England history, but
traditionally overshadowed by the critiques of Puritanism of which it had
so often been a part.

The publication of Harold Stearns's *Liberalism in America* in 1919
played a ground-breaking role in this recovery of secular liberalism by
synthesizing the prewar dialectical analyses of the American past and giving to the spirit of liberal democracy a history distinct from Puritanism.
Stearns accepted Brooks's and Santayana's analysis of the dialectical development of Puritanism under the impact of pioneering, supplementing it
with Mencken's and Bourne's elaboration of Neo-Puritanism and the role
of the will to power. He added, however, that throughout United States
history an alternative, not a derivative, source of wisdom and values had
existed: "from almost the very day of the landing of the first settler the
Puritan fanaticism was tempered by a conflicting liberal spirit." In the area
of reform, American liberals had been sorely tempted to adopt the Neo-
Puritan practice of "enforced meliorism," but otherwise liberalism had
identified itself with the tradition of self-government and voluntarism.[26]

Stearns explicitly wrote *Liberalism in America* to offer the alternative
of nonideological social change to intellectuals beginning to flirt with the
enforced meliorism Russian revolutionary ideology seemed to share with
American Neo-Puritanism. But the terms in which he cast the work had
the more subtle effect of making liberalism a more usable past than Puritanism, an effect that Vernon Louis Parrington later embellished in compelling detail in his panoramic intellectual history *Main Currents of
American Thought*, the first two volumes of which were published in 1927.
Parrington treated Puritanism's highest achievements with respect, but the
theme of his work, like Stearns's, was the rise of American traditions other
than Puritanism and especially the rise of liberalism. By the end of the
decade dissident intellectuals had begun the serious work of authenticating
an American cultural identity both separate from Puritan hegemony and
more useful than Puritanism to the survival and salvation of mass
democracy.[27]

The discovery of a liberal tradition independent of Puritanism,
whether historically valid or not, was essential to the final passing of
the Puritan tradition from the center of America's cultural self-
understanding, more so than either Neo-orthodox Protestant theology or
New Humanism. Not only did liberalism offer an alternative to Puritanism; it also, by definition, made obsolete the process of redefining

---

26 Stearns, *Liberalism in America*, 33, 66.
27 Vernon Louis Parrington, *Main Currents in American Thought* (New York: Harcourt, Brace, & World, 1927).

America's central cultural heritage. The liberal tradition reconstructed during the 1920s was not so much an alternative set of principles, derived from historical rather than transcendent truths, as it was a process, based on the pragmatic method of arriving at public decisions by open discussion and compromise. By embracing liberalism and rejecting Puritanism, American thinkers like Stearns and Parrington did not so much substitute one set of values for another as they completely reoriented their thinking about what was distinctively American. Puritanism now became simply one of many persuasions judged by existing standards of utility. And by its own most recent standard of providing the moral core for the civic culture of mass democracy, it was found wanting because ultimately self-defeating: legislating external control removed the need for inner control as well as the distinction between democratic and authoritarian societies.

The Failure of Puritanism to Redeem History

After the Civil War failed to realize the vision of antebellum Puritan ideology, the product of the other set of circumstances in which American Puritanism and American democracy were closely identified, Puritanism nevertheless enjoyed a reformulation as the genteel tradition. After the 1920s, however, the Puritan tradition never again captured the imagination of intellectuals who saw their responsibility as redefining Puritanism to meet the ongoing challenges confronted by American society and culture, with the possible exception of the publication of Ralph Barton Perry's *Puritanism and Democracy* in 1944. For a decade and a half, the journals and magazines of elevated opinion were devoid of serious debate about the Puritan tradition, aside from reviews of the plethora of scholarly works published in the thirties to correct the many distortions that had crept into the polemics of the preceding decade. As early as the publication of Kenneth Murdock's *Increase Mather: Foremost American Puritan* in 1925, followed rapidly by Samuel Eliot Morison's *Builders of the Bay Colony*, Herbert Schneider's *The Puritan Mind*, Joseph Haroutunian's *Piety versus Moralism: The Passing of New England Theology*, and the first of Perry Miller's studies, *Orthodoxy in Massachusetts, 1630–1650*, the nonscholarly, public discussion of Puritanism was disappearing from the journals. The title of the 1932 *New Republic* review of *Piety versus Moralism*, "The Passing of Puritanism," seemed to symbolize Puritanism's having finally lost its grip on the mind and heart of educated America outside the academy.[28] In stark contrast to Charles Beard's portrayal of the heated debate about Puritanism on the eve of the Plymouth tricentennial in 1920, Samuel Eliot

---

[28] "The Passing of Puritanism," *NR* 72 (October 5, 1932): 214.

Morison was forced to admit in his 1930 *Forum* article, entitled "Those Misunderstood Puritans," that "the recent tercentennial of Massachusetts, the Puritans' pet colony, left the American public completely cold."[29]

The most significant difference between educated conceptions of Puritanism in 1930 and in 1920 was not only the intensity of interest but also a decade's speculation on the relationship of Puritanism to democracy. When such speculation occurred in the 1830s and 1840s, democracy was in the ascent, in the forefront of both national and international development. The reputation of Puritanism benefited from the association with democracy, at least as much as it provided democracy with a moral and historical legitimation. By the 1920s democracy had lost its moral and historical legitimation, despite "winning" the Great War.[30] Its tie with the Puritan theology of history had been broken during the 1880s and 1890s among students of Puritanism, much earlier among more secular-minded Americans. Puritanism not only had nothing to gain from an identification with democracy; it had much to lose and little to give. The severance of Puritan ideals from Puritan history had emasculated the Puritan tradition, leaving it afloat to attract and absorb the anxieties and alienation experienced by turn-of-the-century artists trying to come to terms with modernity. Reunited with the nation's political consciousness in the 1920s, but by only a few threads, the Puritan tradition simply could not survive the association with a democracy whose raison d'etre was the defense of provincialism rather than the redemption of history.

When democracy once again identified itself with the redemption of history during World War II, it is not surprising, then, that Ralph Barton Perry came forward with his classic *Puritanism and Democracy*. More a philosophical than an historical tract, its purpose was "to determine how far the ideals of puritanism and democracy are acceptable." And when Perry discovered that much in the two ideals was not only acceptable but also compatible, he proclaimed them the basis for a renewal of the meaning of Americanism, a revival of faith in what he alternately called puritan democracy, Christian democracy, or moral liberalism.[31] In a comment on the book for the *Saturday Review of Literature*, the historian Allan Nevins compared Perry's contribution with Stuart Sherman's and noted that scholars had long recognized the convergence between Puritanism and democracy in America's history.[32] Other reviewers were not quite as appreciative of Perry's place in historiography, treating

---

[29] Samuel Eliot Morison, "Those Misunderstood Puritans," *Forum* 85 (March 1930): 142.

[30] See especially Edward A. Purcell, Jr., *The Crisis of Democratic Theory* (Lexington, Ky.: Univ. of Kentucky Press, 1973).

[31] Perry, *Puritanism and Democracy*, 43, 630, 634, 638.

[32] Allan Nevins's review, *Saturday Review of Literature* 28 (January 13, 1945): 7.

Puritanism and Democracy instead as at best an act of patriotic faith and at worst a scholastic apologia.[33] Prophetic of what became of the convergence of Puritanism and democracy in the early years of the Cold War, the *New Republic*'s reviewer A. H. Pekelis asserted: "The strongest hope of the world today is in America's ability to be possessed with an idea. But this hope is too precious to be forced into the Procrustean bed of puritanism. Nor, for that matter, should the American ideal ever be reduced to any kind of Americanism."[34] And it was not, at least not in relation to its spiritual roots. In the post–World War II struggle between democracy and communism, democracy has more often than not stood on its own ideological feet. Even during the 1950s, when "godless" or "atheistic" was the most popular description of communism, democracy cultivated its current ecumenical alliances around the globe rather than its past ties to American Puritanism. This may have been in the best spirit of what Perry envisioned for moral liberalism when he concluded his book with the claim: "Americanism . . . consists in a common creed of diversity, adopted by each individual and group because of liberty enjoyed, and because of the fructifying intercourse of multiple liberties. These motives will prompt an American to identify himself with the world-wide and age-long adventure of mankind."[35] But the dropping of the atomic bombs, the end of America's isolationism, and the ensuing four decades of domestic and international tension remind us, on the contrary—as *New Yorker* reviewer Hamilton Basso suggested in 1945— that creeds and ideals are quite different from their application.[36]

---

[33] *Library Journal* 69 (December 15, 1944): 1103; *NR* 112 (April 16, 1945): 520-22; *New Yorker* 20 (January 13, 1945): 74; *Time* 45 (January 22, 1945): 94; *U.S. Quarterly Booklist* 1 (June 1945): 11.

[34] *NR* 112 (April 16, 1945): 522.

[35] Perry, *Puritanism and Democracy*, 641.

[36] *New Yorker* 20 (January 13, 1945): 74.

Index

AOÛT
Boîte oct.
       1 nov
      17 BLN

AVI/10 ET